Waves of Change

A Study of Social Mood

What People Are Saying About

Waves of Change

There's a vibe-shift when it comes to moods. Call them affects, social moods, or just "vibes," we are increasingly aware of how socially connected feelings can affect the economy ("the vibe-cession"), society (the politics of resentment), and even history ("The Summer of Love"). A new book from the vibe-meister himself is thus excellent news; a key manual for navigating the choppy seas of moodshifts and social affects. This is the strategy handbook we need in these moody times.
Alf Rehn, professor of innovation, design, and management, University of Southern Denmark

A book for the times we have lived in, the time we live in and the times we will live in. A book that guides us on a path we believe to be familiar, but a path where we are surprised as to how little we really know about ourselves.
Jeremy Raybould, advisor Lancea Partners, London

Mikko Ketovuori offers a broad, yet insightful, look at socionomics and, in the process, demonstrates the field's applicability to personal and professional decision-making. For those looking for a launch point into the study of social mood and its impact, "Waves of Change" offers a great place to start.
Peter Atwater, adjunct professor in economics, William & Mary; author of *The Confidence Map: Charting a Path from Chaos to Clarity*

In economics, the influence of mood has only recently begun to attract serious attention. This book takes the road less traveled, offering a bold and refreshing perspective that brings culture, pop music, and collective mood into a shared spotlight. It uncovers unexpected patterns that challenge conventional thinking and reveal the hidden rhythms of society. A compelling and thought-provoking read for anyone curious about the deeper forces shaping our world.

Mika Pantzar, professor in consumer society research center, University of Helsinki

The social atmosphere is a vital aspect of any culture or cultural community. It has been already studied by many scholars, but Mikko Ketovuori provides us with a completely new and challenging approach to it — the present global situation of course as its background.

He is in the line of such classics as Heidegger with his notion of Befindlichkeit, the attunement, or Michel Foucault with his episteme... or reflections of Jacques Attali.

In semiotics one speaks of semiosphere as that continuum of signs which guarantees the life of any community to which we want to belong — the mood in society is an existential feeling of a collective agent.

Eero Tarasti, professor emeritus of musicology, Honorary President of the IASS — International Association of Semiotic Studies, University of Helsinki

Dr Ketovuori explores historical events in the context of social mood, illustrating that pre-rational socionomic motivation lies behind diverse types of social actions, from the joyous to the horrific.

Robert R. Prechter, Jr., author of *The Socionomic Theory of Finance*

Waves of Change

A Study of Social Mood

Mikko Ketovuori

IFF
BOOKS

London, UK
Washington, DC, USA

CollectiveInk

First published by iff Books, 2026
iff Books is an imprint of Collective Ink Ltd.,
Unit 11, Shepperton House, 89 Shepperton Road, London, N1 3DF
office@collectiveinkbooks.com
www.collectiveinkbooks.com
www.iff-books.com

For distributor details and how to order please visit the 'Ordering' section on our website.

ISBN: 978 1 917991 61 2 (Paperback)
978 1 917991 67 4 (ebook)
Library of Congress Control Number: 2025945374

A CIP catalogue record for this book is available from the British Library.

Design: Lapiz Digital Services

UK: Printed and bound by CPI Group (UK) Ltd, Croydon, CR0 4YY
Printed in North America by CPI GPS partners

The manufacturer's authorised representative in the EU for product safety is:
eucomply OÜ - Pärnu mnt 139b-14, 11317 Tallinn, Estonia,
hello@ eucompliancepartner.com,
www.eucompliancepartner.com

Previous books by Mikko Ketovuori

(2007) *Two Cultures of Arts Education, Finland and Canada? An Integrated View.* Annales Universitatis Turkuensis, University of Turku.
ISBN 978-951-29-3380-8

(2022) *Laumavaiston varassa.* Agile Publishing, Espoo.
ISBN 978-952-69579-4-4

(2024) *Socionomics: How Social Mood Shapes Society.* Routledge, London.
ISBN 978-1-032-48069-5

For Heli — my wife and muse

Men, it has been well said, think in herds; it will be seen that they go mad in herds, while they only recover their senses slowly, one by one.

Charles Mackay

Contents

Preface

What if our histories, our cultures, our politics, even our financial markets were not haphazard occurrences? What if the evolution of humanity was not merely a collection of random events, but instead the result of predictable cycles of the shifts in collective emotions?

This book looks to reveal the hidden forces behind humanity's progression — and regression — throughout time. Our need to be recognized through cultural identity, the swings in our political compasses, financial booms — and busts. *Waves of Change* identifies how the ebb and flow of social mood dictates likely events rather than events dictating social mood.

By recognizing these patterns, it is possible to see the world a whole new way. As social mood is the collective emotional state that drives trends, crises, and opportunities, it's not just a reaction to events — it *creates* them. This book explores:

- Market psychology — How waves of optimism and pessimism shape financial markets.
- Cultural and political shifts — Why music, fashion, and governance change in cycles.
- Hidden indicators — What the hemline and skyscraper indexes reveal about society.
- History's roadmap — How past social moods foretell the future.

Since we live in an era of uncertainty, the patterns of social mood provide clarity. Whether you're an investor, historian, or simply curious about the world, *Waves of Change* offers a powerful framework for anticipating what's coming next!

Introduction

Do you feel that uncertainty has become a defining feature of our lives? Are you irritated and exhausted by the constant stream of troubling news? If so, you're not alone. A pervasive sense of instability now stretches across communities, nations, and generations. Fear of the future, frustration, and distrust have become widespread. Conversations often devolve into battlegrounds, and civil discourse gives way to emotional polarization. Even if we weren't confused or disoriented, we would still be caught in the sweeping tides of change.

In Europe, the list of ongoing crises is long. War, once a distant fear, is again a reality. Attitudes toward immigration have shifted from openness to restriction. Economic instability fuels cultural division, while populist and nationalist movements gain ground, eroding trust in EU institutions. Could Brexit have been just the beginning? In Eastern Europe, the war in Ukraine, now in its third year, continues to evolve. Reports of North Korean troops in the conflict stir fears of escalation, while Finland and Sweden's NATO accession signals a new geopolitical era. Across the Atlantic, division defines the United States. Some see renewal; others see collapse. Echoes of the 1960s reverberate — civil rights struggles, anti-war protests — but are today's upheavals driven by similar forces?

Perhaps not completely. One key difference is where and how our discourse now unfolds. In the past, it took place in streets, on campuses, and in living rooms. Today, it's mostly online. A digital thumbs-up or down masquerades as engagement. Social media amplifies conflict, simplifies complexity and blurs the boundary between truth and illusion. Emotions now often overpower facts. This is not just disinformation — it's *mood distortion*. To navigate today's turbulent world, we need more than knowledge. We need perspective — the ability to see from a thoughtful distance. That is what this book offers. As the ancient adage goes: *What has been, will be again; there is nothing new under the sun*. History echoes. If we listen carefully, we may begin to understand the present.

The thesis of this book is simple yet radical: Social mood — inherent, collective, and dominant — shapes society and is reflected in global events. But the arrow of causality does **not** run both ways. Events do not shape mood. Rather, mood precedes and influences the events that unfold. This idea runs counter to much of modern thinking. We often believe that historical or political developments drive our emotions. But what if it's the opposite? What if mood drives politics, economics, war, art, and even our daily choices?

In our culture, we are taught that reason rules. The term *Homo sapiens*, "wise man," suggests that rationality defines us. But brain science tells a different story. The neocortex, associated with logic and reasoning, makes up just 10–15 percent of brain volume. The limbic system — responsible for emotion, memory, and social behavior — dominates at 75–80 percent. The reality is, we are emotional creatures first. This book offers a new frame: *Homo sentiens* — feeling human. A being shaped not just by logic but by mood, intuition, memory, and emotion. Our decisions, ideologies, and even historical movements reflect this. Think of Rosa Parks, who defied the prevailing mood of her time not through mimicry but through clarity and conscience. Rare moments like these are not driven by crowd behavior but by something deeper — intelligence as a fusion of intuition, emotion, and reason.

This book expands the ideas introduced in my earlier work, *Socionomics: How Social Mood Shapes Society* (Routledge, 2024), itself inspired by the pioneering ideas of Robert Prechter, founder of the Socionomics Institute and Elliott Wave International. While that work explored the theoretical foundations of socionomics, this book is a more personal and expansive journey. It does not strictly follow socionomic models or stock market analysis but instead charts the cyclical patterns of human society more broadly.

You don't need prior knowledge of socionomics to engage with this book. Through essays grounded in history, psychology, culture, and current affairs, you will encounter compelling evidence of how mood moves the world.

The topics we will explore are:

- How pop music, cinema, fashion, and architecture mirror collective sentiment.
- The lingering trauma of war across generations.
- The rise and fall of ideologies, from communism to technocracy.
- Humanity's recurring urge to censor, control, and compete ideologically.
- The role of technology and media in shaping our emotional climate.
- The cycles of economic manias and crashes that reflect deeper emotional undercurrents.

At the heart of each topic lies a profound question: If mood governs more than we think, how else might our worldview — our sense of reason, progress, even selfhood — be flawed or incomplete? Is social mood really that important? Yes — because it quietly underpins the systems we think we understand:

- Economics. Optimistic moods spur spending; pessimistic ones trigger saving and recession.
- Politics: Good moods elect hopeful leaders; bad moods welcome radicalism.
- Culture: Mood shapes the arts, norms, and spirit of the age.

- Relationships: Collective mood seeps into everyday interactions, either bonding or breaking us.
- Geopolitics: Mood shifts predict conflict and peace with surprising accuracy.

Perhaps this sounds speculative. But once you begin reading, you'll start thinking differently. However, this book is not about abstract theory. It's about the hidden emotional tides that move people, nations, and eras. That is why this book should not just be read, it should be felt! Let yourself be carried by the waves. I promise you may never look at history, politics, or even your own decisions the same way again!

Ten Theses on Social Mood

1. Social mood is a shared state of mind that fluctuates in time dynamically between optimism and pessimism. In its nature the social mood is endogenous, collective, pre-conscious and a-rational. Nothing "impacts" social mood, rather its trends and changes enfold naturally.
2. Since a-rational and non-rational thinking differ qualitatively from rational and irrational thinking, people who act non-rationally base their actions on an intuitive impulse to follow the herd.
3. Mood-motivated decisions are non-rational, but people generate rationalizations to justify them after the fact.
4. Social mood is always present in society.
5. Social mood influences changes in a society's political discourse, attitudes and values.
6. Social mood is unremembered and, without a socionomic perspective, often left unnoticed. That is why certain societal phenomena are repeated time after time: "We learn from history that we do not learn from history."

7. Social mood is reflected in the events, news and atmosphere of the society. In the aggregate, it affects how we spend our time, the things we believe in, as well as the things that draw our attention.
8. When social mood reaches extremes, correspondingly extreme social events follow. Similarly, as the social mood trend becomes less extreme, so do the tenor and character of corresponding events and trends.
9. Social mood influences the kinds of technologies that society creates and embraces, along with society's uses of existing technology.
10. Social mood cannot be altered, but an individual can learn to act in a manner that deviates from prevailing trends.

Chapter 1

It All Starts with Pop Music

The times, they are a-changin'.

— **Bob Dylan**

In 1975, a young and passionate music enthusiast and stock analyst working on Wall Street had a life-changing realization. Just a few years prior, Robert Prechter had graduated from Yale University with a degree in psychology. He was driven by a desire to merge his interests in finance and market behavior. While searching for a way to intertwine these two passions, he located the rare manuscripts of Ralph Nelson Elliott (1871–1948), titled *The Wave Principle* (1938) and *Nature's Law — the Secret of the Universe* (1946). According to Elliott, stock market prices, which often appear random and unpredictable, actually form distinct wave-like structures. These patterns can be used to anticipate fluctuations in stock prices.

While Elliott's theory seemed to be at least practical, it prompted deeper questions: What exactly did these waves signify? Do they have some kind of connection to human emotions? In a moment of serendipity, Prechter realized where he had time after time encountered similar kinds of waves — during the sessions with his rock band, while he was playing the drums, or in his leisure time, when he was listening to popular music! This epiphany would later become a cornerstone in his groundbreaking work, bridging financial theory with cultural analysis, known as socionomics. As he himself remembers that moment in detail and clearly:

I was perusing a wall chart of the stock market and thinking about the tonal changes in Beatles records that occurred in

> *1965–1966. That led me to thinking about popular music in general, which I knew very well. I suddenly perceived that the musical styles I knew about had ebbed and flowed with the stock market. That's when I first had the feeling that I had perceived something important.*[1]

During the 1960s, The Beatles had skyrocketed to unprecedented global fame, first captivating audiences in Britain, then conquering the United States, and eventually enchanting the entire world. This meteoric rise was accompanied by a cultural phenomenon known as Beatlemania, which encapsulated the fervent frenzy and widespread admiration that surrounded the band. The excitement surrounding The Beatles was palpable, with fans erupting into ecstatic screams at their concerts. These outbursts were often so thunderous that the musicians even struggled to hear their own instruments, a testament to the overwhelming passion and energy of their audiences.

Beatlemania wasn't just a craze; it was a movement that defined a generation and left an indelible mark on the history of music. Comprised of the iconic quartet – John Lennon, Paul McCartney, George Harrison, and Ringo Starr – The Beatles transcended their roles as mere musicians to ignite a cultural revolution. Their innovative and infectious music resonated profoundly with young audiences who embraced them as emblems of liberation and self-expression. The Beatles' distinctive hairstyles and charismatic personas catapulted them to instant stardom, influencing global fashion trends and social behaviors. In its entirety, their music and style manifested the entire mood of the 1960s, capturing the essence of the era.

Prechter's observations highlighted a fascinating correlation: as social mood improved, so did The Beatles' success and stock market valuations. From 1963 to 1965, as the market soared, so too did The Beatles' fame, with hit after hit capturing the mood of an optimistic generation. Yet, as social mood soured and the stock market faltered in 1966, The Beatles faced setbacks, including controversies and declining reception. However, it wasn't just about the band's popularity; Prechter's in-depth analysis delved into their music, examining the tone and lyrical content that defined their unique sound — and the mood music. The ebb and flow of public sentiment and market trends not only shaped The Beatles' commercial success and fame but also influenced the evolution of their musical creations. As these external factors shifted, so too did the style and substance of the music they produced, reflecting a dynamic interaction between the band and the world around them!

Two decades later, Robert Prechter embarked on a profound exploration of the complex interconnections between societal moods, financial market trends, and the evolution of popular culture, including music and fashion. This journey began with his 1985 essay, *Popular Culture and The Stock Market*, and Prechter continued to revisit these themes throughout his career, most notably in his 1999 book, *The Wave Principle of Human Social Behavior and the New Science of Socionomics*. Whether delving into the realms of fashion, colors, hairstyles, or examining the themes of popular movies, sports, entertainment, or humor — essentially any sphere where human creativity is expressed — socionomic analyses are conducted today.

Of all the expressions of human life, however, it was music that came to reveal the connection between collective emotion and the mood of the era. These findings do not really come as a surprise to most music researchers. Music, indeed, stands as the closest reflection of human emotions and thus reflects the moods of the era too. As a universal language, music is able to evoke deep collective emotions as well as individual feelings instantaneously, without the need for any words. How fascinating this is! But what was the mood?

The clearest description of the mood in society can be found from John Casti's book *Mood Matters,* where he defines social mood as the collective beliefs of a population about their expected future. These beliefs greatly shape a society's development and culture. In his book, Casti outlines four phases of social mood – mood rising, mood peak, mood declining and mood bottom – each of them linked to an emotion: hope, hubris, fear, and despair. From these hope and fear are the most common emotions.

Table 1. **The taxonomy of moods by Casti (2010, p. 25).**

+ Mood rising	**+ Mood peak**	**– Mood declining**	**– Mood bottom**
Hope	Hybris	Fear	Despair

As Casti notes, extreme fluctuations in social mood – whether exceedingly optimistic or pessimistic – are uncommon occurrences. For this reason, projecting the continuation of the current trend, whether it be on an upward or downward trajectory, tends to be a reliable forecast. In other words: tomorrow will be like today. The true challenge, however, is in predicting those crucial inflection points where trends begin to reverse. Successfully anticipating these pivotal moments is a highly sought-after expertise, often deserving of significant reward.

In a society, a positive social mood fosters an atmosphere of hope. During this phase, society thrives based on optimism, openness, and tolerance, encouraging people to take risks and strive for success. Since this optimistic phase is not, however, everlasting, eventually the social mood reaches a peak where hubris begins to overshadow hope. At this juncture, the foundational values and principles that once drove success start slowly to erode, leading to a shift toward a negative mood.

As social mood turns negative, society's self-confidence wanes, giving rise to suspicion, fear, polarization and pessimism. This environment fosters discord, mistrust and people start to oppose centrist beliefs, while they seek more extreme ideologies. When the social mood hits a deep negative extreme and despair, it leads to economic downturns, systemic failures, and even conflicts. Yet, at the depth of despair, a new cycle of positive mood has already begun to emerge, offering fresh opportunities and hope for recovery. Does this sound reasonable so far? But how do you prove that Casti's' theory holds true?

My journey into exploring the social mood began with my musical background, almost like Prechter's had earlier. As an all-round musician, I have had the privilege of playing the cello in symphony orchestras, studying music academically and teaching teacher candidates at the university. This rich tapestry of musical experiences cultivated a deep curiosity within me about the underlying forces that shape musical expression and its impact on society.

However, unlike Prechter, whose insights into the connection between music and societal moods were driven by an inductive revelation, my approach was much slower and rooted more in empirical analysis. I was determined to delineate a research framework robust enough to assess the impact of musical moods with precision.

This drove me to develop a central research question that would guide my inquiry: How can different musical tones reflect the mood of different eras? Recognizing that genres of pop music have significantly diverged across decades – most people can differentiate the styles of the 1990s from those of the 1970s or 1980s, for instance – suggested that musical genres themselves may contain meanings that are tied to prevalent social mood. Prechter's video *Histories Hidden Engine*[2] that catches the essence of this idea, suggests that the bright and optimistic tones of music from the early 1960s and the 1980s corresponded to the positive moods of those times. In contrast, the darker tones prevalent in the music of the 1970s align with the negative social moods of that era. The early 1960s and the 1980s were distinguished by periods of economic prosperity and thriving stock markets. In contrast, the 1970s experienced economic stagnation and downturns in financial markets. This raises an intriguing question: what indicators might signal a change in social mood during the peaks and troughs of these fluctuations?

Upon reflection, it seems that if the 1960s were characterized by burgeoning optimism and the 1970s by a period of decline, the iconic Woodstock festival of 1969 could be viewed as a cultural and emotional nexus, capturing the spirit and zeitgeist of the era. Woodstock stands as a powerful symbol of the transformative cultural wave that surged through the middle of these two distinct decades, bridging the hopeful aspirations of the 1960s with the challenging realities that unfolded in the 1970s. As 1960s optimism turned into pessimism, 1970s songs grew more critical, angrier, and eventually disillusioned.

Some songs even became anthems, capturing the mood of the time. "Fortunate Son" by Creedence Clearwater Revival, for example, criticized the Vietnam War, reflecting the growing dissatisfaction among American youth. In its turn, "A Horse With No Name" expressed more introspective disillusionment, with its haunting tune and surreal lyrics suggesting a desire for a simpler, more genuine life, free from societal pressures. While the tide in the early 1980s turned up once again, it was punk rock that characterized the need for the change. Like Woodstock had been a manifestation of the peak of positive mood, at the bottom, *new wave* (literally!) kicked in more creative, more energetic and gradually more joyful music making room for many new musical styles.

If we look at pop music from almost anytime, we can identify these kind of shifts in mood in even shorter periods. For instance, the evolution of pop music in the early 2000s, with the emergence of artists like Britney Spears and *NSYNC, ushered in an era of polished, upbeat, and highly produced music that contrasted sharply with the grunge and alternative rock of the 1990s. This transition signaled a shift towards a more commercial and polished sound, reflecting changes in societal attitudes and consumer preferences. As I pondered these concepts, my research plan began to crystallize.

First, we needed to identify two distinct time periods that contrasted starkly with one another, with one embodying hope and the other embodying fear. Following this, it was essential to develop a straightforward, yet effective measurement tool, capable of reliably assessing musical moods in an experimental environment. Given my Finnish heritage, it seemed only natural to focus our research on Finland's most globally renowned company, the mobile phone behemoth Nokia. As Finland's flagship brand, Nokia achieved unprecedented international success during the 2000s. However, its dominance was short-lived as emerging technologies swiftly claimed the market.

For our study, we chose the years 2006 and 2009 as pivotal reference points from the Nokia stock index — 2006 epitomizing a period of optimism, while 2009 embodied a sense of pessimism. In the summer of 2006, there was a widespread sense of positivity and confidence in the future. Finland was basking in a celebratory mood, highlighted by Lordi's Eurovision victory, triumphs in the Olympics and Ice Hockey World Championships, and the significant rise in Nokia's stock value. However, by 2009 the landscape had changed drastically. Nokia's fortunes had dwindled, and the ripple effects of the financial crisis originating in America had severely impacted the Finnish economy.

Could the music people gravitated toward during these contrasting years mirror a shift also in the mood of the music? In order to prove this, we created a research design that identified a change in societal mood using eight different indicators, including a financial crisis, negative sentiment measures, the rise of radical politics, and the collapse of a mobile business division of Nokia.[3] Preliminary observations of economic indicators, such as the OMX Helsinki Index, Nokia's stock price, and Eurostat's economic sentiment indicator were clear as they all accompanied the Dow Jones industrial average almost identically.

Figure 1. Social mood indicators in Finland

Our hypothesis was that this shift in social mood could also be seen in the increase of pessimism in the pop songs topping the charts in 2009 compared to 2006. To test this, we had to create a tool which could measure optimism and pessimism in music. As previous research had shown that people can accurately identify musical moods, such as depressing, sad, uplifting, optimistic, or enthusiastic, regardless of their musical tastes, we thought that the same phenomenon could also be proven between music and social mood.

To measure musical moods quantitatively, we adapted Casti's "taxonomy of moods" to a frequently used scale in healthcare settings, the Visual Analogue Scale (VAS). Healthcare professionals often employ the VAS to gauge patients' subjective pain experiences, categorizing different types of pain that correspond to the scale's extremes: "no pain" and "worst pain." The VAS, originally developed in the United States in 1921,[4] consists of a continuous horizontal line, usually of 10 cm in printed length, and two descriptive phrases at the two extremities. The scale is commonly ranged from 0 (left, least extreme) to 10 (right, most extreme).

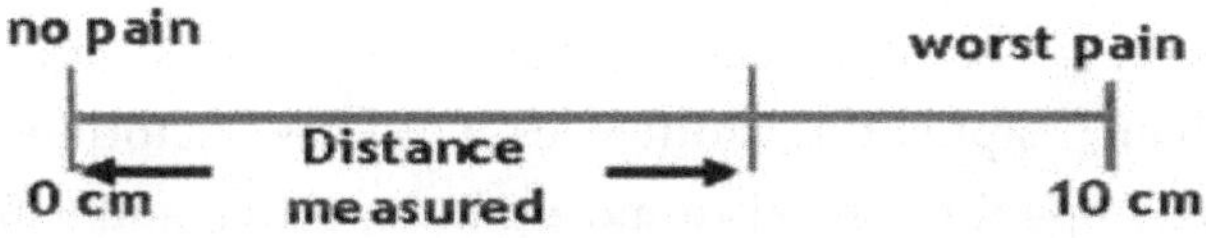

Figure 2. VAS scale

For our specific application, we tailored the scale's two extremes to signify "despair" and "hubris," thus aligning it with the taxonomy of moods. Then we played music tracks from the years 2006 and 2009 to university students and asked them to evaluate and rank these songs using a scale from 0 to 10, where zero signified ultimate despair and ten denoted ultimate hubris. Students were instructed that if they perceived a song as positive, they should assign it a ranking between 5 and 10.

Conversely, if they found a song to be pessimistic, it should receive a score of less than five. Without going further into our research published by Cambridge, the reader may wish to listen to the following four test songs and consider whether they convey the social mood as we interpreted it. The study included four different songs with four emotional states, as follows:

Example of hope, Song 1. Spice Girls: "Wannabe" (*Spice*, 1996). The iconic single "Wannabe" by the legendary girl group Spice Girls stands as one of the bestselling singles by a female ensemble globally. This energetic piece is a vibrant fusion of dance-pop, tinged with elements of rap and hip-hop, delivering an infectious rhythm that captivates listeners. The song radiates an optimistic and hopeful outlook towards the future, resonating with audiences worldwide. It received an impressive average rating of 8.6 from students, reflecting its enduring appeal and positive message.

Example of hubris, Song 2. Queen: "We Are the Champions" (*News of the World*, 1977).
Widely recognized as one of Queen's most iconic anthems, "We Are the Champions" resonates powerfully at sports events around the globe. While the chorus is undeniably catchy and triumphant, captivating audiences with its victorious flair, the song's opening reveals a more introspective and reflective tone. This initial sentiment invites listeners on a journey through a tapestry of emotions, culminating in an uplifting and empowering crescendo. Despite its slightly lower student rating of 8.2 compared to "Wannabe," "We Are the Champions" is a song that represent the moment *after* the victory.

Example of fear, Song 3. Nirvana: "Smells Like Teen Spirit" (*Nevermind*, 1991).
"Smells Like Teen Spirit" is a key song in alternative rock, also called post-punk, grunge, or indie. Known for its cynical and

pessimistic lyrics, it has become one of the most famous tracks of its era, often seen as an anthem for a generation. The song deeply connects with listeners, capturing the rebellious and disillusioned spirit of youth. Reflecting this feeling, students rated the song with a score of 3.8, showing a moderate level of pessimism. Some students found it hard to separate their personal liking for the song from its mood, admitting it isn't a cheerful piece of music.

Example of despair, Song 4. Slipknot: "Psychosocial" (*All Hope Is Gone*, 2008).
The concluding track in the pilot study was delivered by the renowned American heavy metal outfit, Slipknot. The band's music is a fusion of nu metal, thrash metal, and death metal genres, characterized by intense and visceral soundscapes. Slipknot has gained a reputation for their high-octane, chaotic, and often aggressive live performances, which captivate audiences worldwide. Their lyrics frequently delve into themes of nihilism, anger, disaffection, and mental turmoil, often laced with profanity and aggressive undertones. One such example is the music video for the track "Psychosocial," which visually portrays a burning barn and features eerie purgatory masks, further emphasizing the band's dark aesthetic. Overall, the pessimistic tone of their music aligns with the theme of their album, titled *All Hope Is Gone*, delivering on the promise of its title with unrelenting intensity and raw emotion. The average rating of the song was 2.9.

Our expectations were met as the first two songs were perceived as more optimistic than the last two. This prepared us to proceed with the main study, which included songs from both 2006 and 2009. To our surprise, the findings of the study revealed quite clearly that songs from these two different years indeed exhibited different moods.[5] The 2006 songs were characterized by optimism, while the 2009 songs conveyed a sense of pessimism. This suggested that the mood in music is not necessarily tied to specific genres or decades but can fluctuate over shorter spans of time as well.

I then began to ponder where else we might discover comparable indicators of mood and how these emotional states could influence and shape our society. I wanted to explore the basic ideas of the theory and, after that, look into its many uses in different fields. However, I had to first understand the waves that had so greatly inspired Elliott and subsequently influenced Prechter.

1. Prechter, R. R. (2016). *The Socionomic Theory Of Finance*, p. 781.
2. https://youtu.be/DZlH56Bemog?feature=shared
3. Ketovuori, M. and Lampert, M. (2018). From "'Hard Rock Hallelujah' to 'Ukonhauta' in Nokialand – A socionomic perspective on the mood shift in Finland's popular music from 2006 to 2009," *Popular Music 2:* pp. 237– 252.
4. Hayes M. H. S. and Patterson D. G. (1921). "Experimental development of the graphic rating method," *Psychological Bulletin 18*: pp. 98–99.
5. The paired two-sample (each student's average rating for the songs in the 2006 sample versus each student's average rating for the songs in the 2009 sample) t-test showed a statistically significant difference of 2.0764 ($t = 13.9369$, d.f. = 81, one-tailed $p < 0.0001$).

Chapter 2

Mapping Growth and Decline

Understanding of life begins with the understanding of patterns.

— **Fritjof Capra**

Life in Kansas during the 1870s was a vibrant tapestry of hope and hardship. The vast Great Plains enticed settlers with promises of fertile land and new beginnings, driven by the allure of the Homestead Act of 1862. This legislation offered 160 acres of land to anyone willing to cultivate it, attracting a diverse group of pioneers, including immigrants and civil war veterans. Confronted with a scarcity of timber, these resourceful newcomers constructed "soddies" — sod houses built from the very earth they tilled. Although these modest dwellings provided essential shelter, they left their inhabitants vulnerable to the harsh and unpredictable Kansas weather.

Additionally, the year 1874 saw the arrival of the infamous "Grasshopper Plagues," a devastating onslaught that ravaged crops and posed severe challenges to the fledgling communities. Contemporary accounts describe swarms of locusts that descended upon the land, spending days stripping fields and trees bare, even invading farmers' homes to consume stored food before moving on. Inside homes, carpets and clothing were not spared, while outdoors the insects' excrement and carcasses fouled ponds and streams. The sky darkened with the sheer number of locusts, casting a pall over the land as if it were winter. Despite these adversities, the settlers displayed remarkable resilience and unity, steadfastly clinging to their visions of a prosperous future. Kansas was both geographically and symbolically the heart of America, embodying values such as hard work, resilience, and independence.

It was from this rich, cultural and historical backdrop that Ralph Nelson Elliott was born in Marysville in 1871. When Ralph was 9, his family, including his parents and older sister, relocated to San Antonio, Texas, where he learned to read and write Spanish fluently. In 1891, he moved to Mexico to work on the railroads as a lineman, train dispatcher, stenographer, and station agent. During those days, many jobs were learned through apprenticeships and on-the-job experiences. Although it is unclear how Elliott transitioned into an accountant (and later an executive) at several railroad companies in Mexico, as well as Central and South America, he demonstrated an unyielding determination to master the basics of the field and its practices independently.

Like many other self-taught individuals of his era, Elliott was undoubtedly a detail-oriented, disciplined, and resilient thinker. Having acquired his knowledge of railway practices through hands-on experience, he likely developed a keen understanding of accounting as well. Elliott took the initiative to reorganize accounting methods, aligning them with the emerging principles of his time. This included implementing new systems of record keeping, anticipating future expenses, and effectively allocating revenues.

It is also probable that at that time Elliott became first acquainted with the foundational accounting principles introduced by Luca Pacioli (1447–1517). Another of Pacioli's works, *De Divina Proportione,* which featured illustrations by Leonardo da Vinci, explores the concept of the Golden Ratio.[6] Without the insights provided by this seminal book, Elliott might not have developed his wave theory later in his life (I will return to this issue later in the book in concluding remarks).

Amidst the turbulent climate of civil unrest in Mexico and mounting anti-American sentiment, President Woodrow

Wilson took decisive action in 1916 by ordering the evacuation of US citizens from the country. This directive prompted Elliott and his wife to relocate to Los Angeles, California, where they reunited with his parents and sister, who had previously moved from San Antonio. However, shortly after the family reunion, Elliott and his wife packed their belongings and journeyed to New Jersey, before eventually settling in the bustling metropolis of New York City. While their precise motivations for relocating remain somewhat enigmatic, it is plausible that the move was influenced by the fact that Elliott's wife hailed from New York, with family ties nearby in New Jersey.

During his tenure in New York, Elliott assumed the role of editor for the business magazine, *Tea Room and Gift Shop*. In this capacity, he authored insightful columns offering advice on the financial intricacies of running tea rooms, such as the advantages of incorporating a business. Elliott's columns delved into the principles of "scientific management," advocating for its potential to enhance profitability. He provided guidance to entrepreneurs, identifying prevalent issues such as inadequate financial records and underscoring the importance of sound accounting practices. Elliott boldly asserted that the primary causes of business failure stem from excessive debt, insufficient capital, lack of experience, and poor record keeping. He advised aspiring business owners to pursue industries they are passionate about and to gain diverse experience by working in various roles within their chosen field, echoing his own career journey.

In 1924, Ralph Nelson Elliott embarked on a new chapter as the Chief Accountant for Nicaragua under the auspices of the US State Department. Unfortunately, his tenure in Central America took a toll on his health, as he contracted a debilitating tropical disease, resulting in chronic fever, dysentery, and significant weight loss. By 1929, he was further afflicted by pernicious anemia, which left him severely fatigued. To compound his personal struggles, the stock market crash of 1929 ushered in a period of economic turmoil. For many, such setbacks might have signaled the end of their engagement and curiosity. Some might have even succumbed to despair, but Elliott saw a remarkable opportunity. If he could no longer work in his traditional sense, he resolved to immerse himself in study. For years, numbers had been his realm, with balance sheets, audits, and corporate ledgers structuring his daily life. Now he began to meticulously study and model the movements of the Dow Jones Industrial Average over its 75-year history.

Armed with just a pen, paper, and a ruler, he dove into the seemingly chaotic world of the stock market. In the beginning, the financial markets seemed to be a whirlwind of chaos, an incessant fluctuation with no apparent order. However, as Elliott immersed himself further and accumulated more data, he discerned something remarkable: contrary to initial impressions, markets were not random, *they moved in waves!* Elliott's theory proposed that stock prices follow predictable patterns influenced by human psychology, rather than being random. He believed these patterns affect all areas of life, impacting growth and decline.

After Elliott, it was Robert Prechter who dedicated his life to exploring this theory further, aiming to clarify and answer its questions about the cyclical nature of reality. His work sought to demonstrate the practical power of Elliott's ideas, not just in theory but in real-world financial markets. This became evident in the 1980s when Prechter's Elliott Wave-based predictions gained widespread recognition, accurately foreseeing the decade's roaring bull market. His prescient warning ahead of the 1987 stock market crash further cemented his influence, earning him a place among the most respected analysts of his time. At a period when fundamental analysis dominated Wall Street, Prechter championed a different perspective — one that focused on crowd psychology, mass sentiment, and cyclical patterns as the primary drivers of financial markets. Some of his later bearish predictions, particularly regarding long-term deflationary trends, diverged sharply from actual market behavior, leading to debate among financial professionals.

Just as Elliott extensively relied on his personal experiences and insights from observing small businesses to develop his wave theory, Prechter's intellectual foundation was similarly rooted in practical observation. In Prechter's case, his firsthand experiences and keen observations while trading on Wall Street mirrored the patterns he had discerned from Elliott's work. A striking example of this can be found in his depiction of the trading floors, where he vividly captures the exhilarating and dynamic atmosphere among stock traders, conveying the vibrant energy that permeates these bustling environments:

Let's say that there has been a bear market going on for a week. Now, to a pit trader, that's a major bear market: five straight trading days of declining prices, with small rallies along the way. It's already worn him out. One day, the traders are watching the tape, and it's kind of slow because volume has receded during the decline. Suddenly, the market seems to be stalled out. A couple of traders who have been there the longest, you know, the grizzled old guys that really know the game, who have been there for almost two whole years, are watching the tape from the back of the room, and they say, "buy me ten, buy me fifty, buy me a hundred."

A few heads turn because these are pretty good-sized lots. Sure enough, the market starts to tick up a little bit. Then it stops again and starts to recede very slowly. Most people are saying, "Ah, it's the same old stuff, a rally and a decline; it's going to come back to new lows just like it's been doing for a week. Forget it." They take another bite of their sandwiches and keep half an eye on the board. This is the point of lethargy and conviction that marks a second wave. Soon they notice that the market isn't making a new low; it's holding at a higher bottom. Well, to traders, that's a fundamental news event.

They start watching more closely, and all of a sudden, they get a bit excited, and one or two orders pop out. Then the floodgates open. They are screaming and yelling buy orders, and sure enough, prices are roaring up. It's a broad, powerful third wave. It goes on for a full minute and a half but ends abruptly, and another reaction sets in. Guys who bought late have a small loss. It is the fourth wave's "surprising disappointment."

Now, behind the scenes, over in the corner, there are some younger traders, who have been trading for only about week and a half. They have been keeping an eye on this action, saying to themselves, "Man, look at that wild move! Look at the money we could have made just then! If I'd only been long! I tell you what, if this market starts up again one more time, I'm gonna buy. I'm getting ready." They're watching closely, eyes riveted on the board. Sure enough, the market starts up again. Those young guys start to yell in their orders: "Buy me one! Buy me one!" The market jumps to a new high. Orders from Merrill Lynch finally make it down to the floor, ending as the fifth wave culminates. The old guys who started it all croak from the back, "Sell me ten, sell me fifty, sell me hundred," and the five-wave move is over.[7]

The activity on the trading floor is a compelling demonstration of how the short-term, classic Elliott Wave pattern occurs in the real world. This pattern is distinguished by a sequence of five ascending waves, punctuated by two brief corrective waves. After the market reaches its peak, it typically transitions into a corrective phase, highlighting the cyclical nature of market movements, as depicted in Figure 3.

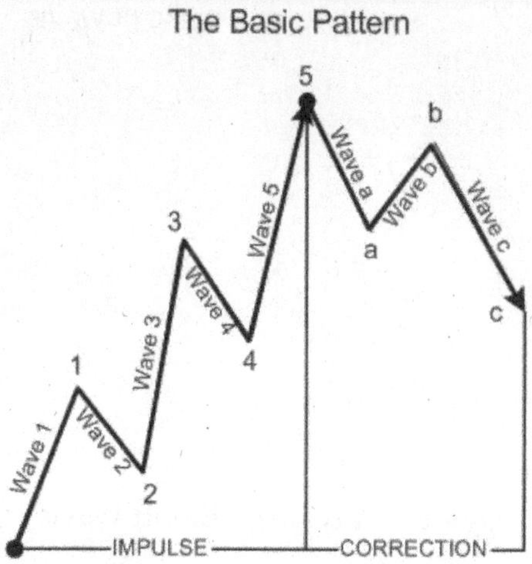

Figure 3. The basic wave pattern

In this example, it may initially seem that the impulsive waves are spurred by enthusiastic, less experienced traders who are pushing the market upward. On the other hand, seasoned traders, armed with extensive experience, are thought to predict these movements and subsequently steer the market towards correction. However, it's crucial to understand that no single individual or group truly controls these events. According to Prechter, the trading frenzy is an emergent phenomenon influenced by the social mood of all participants. No single person or group orchestrates this process; rather, *social mood* is the driving force behind these events. Traders, as a collective, are swept along by the ebb and flow of this mood, forming *a herd* and following their herding instinct. In other words, social mood goes beyond what each person brings to the group. It comes from people copying each other without realizing it. This leads to a group behavior that is neither planned nor even expected!

Even though the foundational Elliott Wave model is straightforward, its application in real-world scenarios is, of course, much more complex. The basic pattern of the Elliott Wave in a real-life setting might look like the iterations in Figure 4.

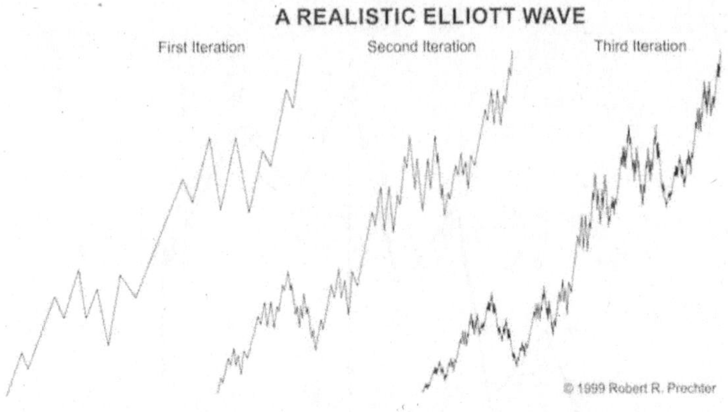

Figure 4. A realistic Elliott Wave

The Elliott Wave Principle is easy to understand. Here's a basic pattern using a rising price scenario:

- Wave one: The market sentiment is negative, but some buyers appear, causing prices to start rising. Public involvement is limited.
- Wave two: Prices fall back but don't go below the start of wave one. News is often negative, sometimes more so than at the beginning of wave one.
- Wave three: This is usually the strongest wave with more positive news. Prices rise steadily, and more people start participating.
- Wave four: This is a corrective wave, allowing those who missed earlier opportunities to buy as prices pull back.
- Wave five: The trend reaches its peak. The market becomes overpriced, and the public buys heavily, but a trend change is likely as the market weakens technically.

The core of Elliott's theory suggests that market prices unfold in specific patterns known as waves. These waves are fractal in nature, meaning they are self-similar across different time scales. To understand how fractals are formed in the Elliott Wave model, consider the following pattern:

1. Minute Waves: These are the smallest observable waves, occurring over very short periods like minutes. They reflect the immediate market reactions and are the building blocks of larger wave structures.
2. Hourly and Daily Waves: As we zoom out, minute waves combine to form larger patterns visible on hourly and daily charts. These waves capture more extended market moves, showing trends and corrections over significant timeframes.
3. Monthly Waves: On a monthly scale, hourly and daily waves aggregate into even larger formations. These waves represent major market cycles, showing long-term trends and reversals.

To sum it up, Elliott Waves consist of five-wave patterns in the direction of the main trend and three-wave patterns in the corrective phase. This structure repeats across all timeframes, creating a fractal pattern — a pattern of growth and decline. Similar to the intricacies of tree branches or the undulating lines of coastal shorelines, fractals in nature also manifest in the delicate symmetry of snowflakes, the spiral patterns of galaxies, and the repetitive structures of Romanesco broccoli.

However, in practice and by the narrowest definition of all, the Elliott Wave model allows traders to analyze market behavior consistently, regardless of the timeframe. Each wave, whether minute or monthly, adheres to the same fundamental principles, showcasing the repetitive and fractal characteristics of market movements.

While Prechter's observations from the Wall Street trading floor example probably took about five minutes, the market waves occur and are on the move all the time in different layers.

The eye of a skilled market analyst can discern these fractal patterns despite the chaos and confusion that reality conceals. When superimposed, the various periodic wave movements form a larger trend, which, as music (if waves could be played!), resembles a fugue. The periods of growth and decline form a beautiful whole, as depicted in this picture below.

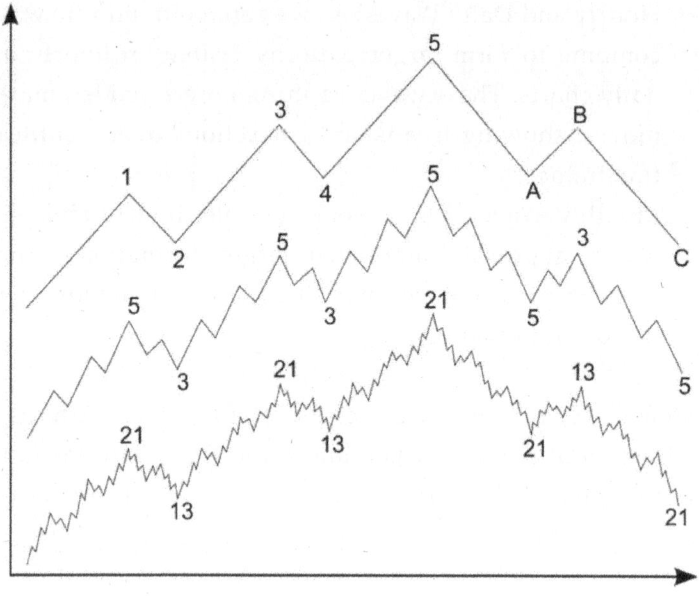

Figure 5. "The fugue of waves"

By leveraging the intricate principles and guidelines of the Elliott Wave Principle, seasoned traders can make informed and probabilistic predictions about market trends and future movements. Mastery of Elliott Waves extends beyond mere theoretical knowledge; it requires a profound, experiential understanding that seamlessly blends analytical insights with practical application. This elevated level of expertise empowers traders to navigate the complexities of the market with heightened precision and confidence, enabling them to interpret and anticipate future market dynamics with remarkable effectiveness.

While delving into the nuances of the theory and its technical intricacies can be complex, the Elliott Wave Principle has undoubtedly established itself as a reliable tool for a diverse array of investors and portfolio managers globally. Often employed alongside other technical analysis techniques, it aids in predicting market movements and identifying lucrative trading opportunities. What many might not realize, however, is that the related socionomic theory also offers the ability to forecast changes in society; and sometimes even more so.

In 2022, I encountered an intriguing development while authoring my inaugural book *Laumavaiston varassa* in Finnish. To my surprise, the content I crafted unfolded in ways I could never have predicted...

6. While Elliott met Charles J. Collins later around 1939, it was Collins' who introduced Elliott to the idea of the fusion of wave principle and the Fibonazzi sequence (Bolton 2018, p. 16).
7. Prechter, R. (1999). *The Wave Principle of Human Social Behavior and the New Science Of Socionomics*, pp. 220–221.

Chapter 3

The Winds and Waves of War

What is the cause of historical events? Power. What is power? Power is the sum total of wills transferred to one person. On what condition are the wills of the masses transferred to one person? On condition that the person express the will of the whole people. That is, power is power. That is, power is a word the meaning of which we do not understand.

— ***War and Peace,* Leo Tolstoy**

When newcomers from abroad arrive at a bar in Helsinki, they are likely to hear some version of this same story, usually shared by men while sipping a beer: in order to really understand Finland, you have to know how its history has been profoundly shaped by its geographical and political position between East and West.

In the early nineteenth century, one of the key moments of Finnish history was when Finland transitioned from Swedish to Russian control following the events of Napoleon's invasion of Russia. This change resulted in Finland being designated as an autonomous Grand Duchy in 1815. In the nineteenth century, when Finland was more of an idea than a real country, the idea of independence smoldered in the background, along with other romantic European nationalist sentiments. During World War I, Finland saw the opportunity to declare its independence in 1917.

However, gaining independence was not that easy, as the country descended into civil war. The conflict was fought between the Reds, who were supported by Bolshevik Russia, and the Whites, who looked for help from Germany. The aftermath of the Russian Revolution further strained Finland's relations with the emerging Soviet Union, shrouding their interactions in suspicion and hostility. The previously porous eastern boundary was now a tightly sealed frontier (just like it is today, by the way). When the storm of World War II descended upon Europe, Finland initially aspired to remain neutral.

In 1939, after the outbreak of World War II, Germany and the Soviet Union forged the infamous Molotov-Ribbentrop Pact. This agreement delineated spheres of influence and placed Finland, along with the eastern regions of Poland and the Baltic states, under Soviet dominion. Immediately after the treaty, Stalin began to make territorial demands on his neighboring countries. Even though the Soviets pretended to negotiate in Moscow, Finland refused to give up any land to them. This disagreement led to the start of the Winter War on November 30, 1939.

The Soviet Union orchestrated a surprise offensive, utilizing the fabricated Mainila incident as a pretext – erroneously alleging that Finnish forces had struck first. The Soviet onslaught commenced with a relentless barrage of artillery. When Russian bombers flew over Helsinki, some residents even ran to open spaces, waving their arms to show "we are here, please don't bomb us!," illustrating the disbelief among some Finns, who couldn't imagine that anyone would attack their country.

In December 1939, during the Red Army's attack, Finnish defenders, although outnumbered, showed great courage and clever tactics. The severe winter, with temperatures dropping to minus 40°C, worked in their favor. Finnish soldiers, skilled in skiing, moved quickly across the snow, while Russian troops struggled in the deep snow. Using the so-called "Motti tactics," the Finns agilely navigated the snow, breaking the enemy into smaller groups, thus overcoming their larger numbers. The cruel saying: *one Finn is equal to ten Russians*, refers to the ratio in which 140,000 Russian soldiers are estimated to have died in three months, while during the same time period approximately 27,000 Finns fell (if we do the math the ratio is in fact 5.3; but why spoil a good story?).

The Winter War persisted for 105 arduous days, but eventually, the Finnish forces faced critical shortages in manpower and supplies, necessitating a tactical withdrawal. This predicament culminated in the signing of the Moscow Peace Treaty in March 1940. However, the war was far from over at this point. As German Chancellor Adolf Hitler observed Finland's staunch resistance against Soviet aggression, he made a critical miscalculation by underestimating the military prowess of the Soviet Union.

In 1941, when Operation Barbarossa was set in motion, Finland found itself aligning with Germany to once again challenge the Soviet Union, driven by the desire to reclaim the territories lost in Karelia. This alliance with the Germans was almost an unavoidable decision for Finland, given its substantial dependence on military supplies. Meanwhile, the British and other Western powers, preoccupied with their own challenges, had already demonstrated their inability to assist Finland during the Winter War of 1939.

Despite the presence of German forces in the north of Finland, Lapland, who aimed to sever Western aid flowing to Murmansk in Finland, maintained its autonomy and operated independently under the leadership of Marshal Mannerheim, the Commander-in-Chief of the Finnish Army. A significant demonstration of this was Mannerheim's decisive prohibition of Finnish troops from participating in the Siege of Leningrad. The alliance between Finland and Germany eventually unraveled between 1944 and 1945, culminating in Finland negotiating an armistice with the Soviet Union. Subsequently, Finland redirected its military efforts against Germany during the so-called Lapland War. Remarkably, despite being ensnared between the proverbial "plague and cholera" — Nazi Germany and the Soviet Union — Finland successfully preserved its sovereignty.

My grandparents, whose ancestral roots lay in the east, now-lost land of Karelia, seldom spoke about the war.

My grandmother would often brush off the past with her characteristically sarcastic remark, *A Russian is a Russian, even if it's fried in butter.* My grandfather, a sergeant who fought along the storied Battle of Kollaa river, was similarly reticent about his wartime experiences. He often recounted the words of his company commander, Aarne Juutilainen: *you do not retreat from these defensive positions, you either hold them or die.* The company commander, Juutilainen, earned the fearsome moniker "The terror of Morocco" due to his distinguished service in the French Foreign Legion across the African continent. This reputation was further cemented by a notorious incident where, in a moment of uncontrolled fury, he shot a young officer in the leg for failing to follow orders promptly during a meal.

Among the ranks, serving under the lead Lieutenant, was the legendary marksman Simo Häyhä, famously dubbed the "White Death" for his unparalleled skills as a sniper. If you go to bars nowadays in Warsaw and you tell people that you're from Finland, people will probably excitedly mention the name "Simo Häyhä" to you... I wonder, what the reason might be, do you?

Following the tumultuous period of the war, Juutilainen, like many of his comrades, found it challenging to adjust to the peacetime, eventually succumbing to alcoholism. During that era, therapeutic interventions were not commonly available or widely practiced. The shared trauma of war left a profound impact on Finnish families, leading to a pervasive atmosphere of silence and poor communication within homes. These behavioral tendencies, often linked to Finnish identity, have their origins in the social mood shaped by the war-torn generation. This legacy of silence and emotional restraint has been passed down, subtly influencing the lives of subsequent generations, including their children and grandchildren. Fortunately, the fourth younger generation in Finland is already living in a different era in this regard.

It's truly fascinating, and somewhat paradoxical, how people recount these kind of war stories in such a uniform manner. These narratives seem to transcend time, weaving a common thread through generations, as they awaken a collective consciousness and endow it with emotional significance, shaping cultural identity. This type of endogenous sharing of meaning exemplifies the essence of social mood: a subconscious remembrance of the emotions our ancestors once felt.

Perhaps, fear and its accompanying aggression, though deeply ingrained in human nature, are the most underestimated forces that propel the course of historical events. These collective emotions serve as a clear reflection of social mood and frequently lead to profound outcomes, including the outbreak of wars. Since social mood often remains unnoticed, these social phenomena tend to repeat themselves throughout history, which — indeed — then repeats itself.

And that's what it really seems to do. In February 2022, I came up with the fascinating insight that the Elliott Wave Principle has extraordinary potential to predict phenomena through social mood. I witnessed the war in Ukraine a month before it began. The difference between optimistic and pessimistic times can be strikingly different.

In 1989, when the Berlin Wall came down, the sense of hope for a brighter future was literally tangible. It was a time when many believed that the ideals of Western liberalism would permeate Eastern Europe, unlocking new opportunities and freedom for millions. Even Russia, once a formidable adversary, was viewed as a potential ally. During this transformative period, there were even genuine discussions about Russia joining NATO, highlighting concerted efforts to mend fences and foster cooperation between erstwhile foes.

The era was characterized by an overwhelming desire to integrate into the global community and embrace Western democratic ideals, promoting unprecedented unity and collaboration across the continent. However, fast-forward, and much like the unexpected collapse of the Soviet Union, the current dynamics with Russia caught many off guard. Those who dare to challenge dominant narratives often find themselves in the margins or not heard at all. In prosperous times, pessimistic forecasters are frequently sidelined, yet when adversity strikes, few possess the foresight to envision a path toward improvement.

Reflecting on the *fried-butter* wisdom imparted by my grandmother, I, along with some fellow Finns of mine, harbored reservations about our eastern neighbor. As I was studying Elliott Waves and socionomics, my suspicions were however, not based on mere intuition, but rather on research-based facts that supported the pessimistic view. The chart that I was staring at looked like this.

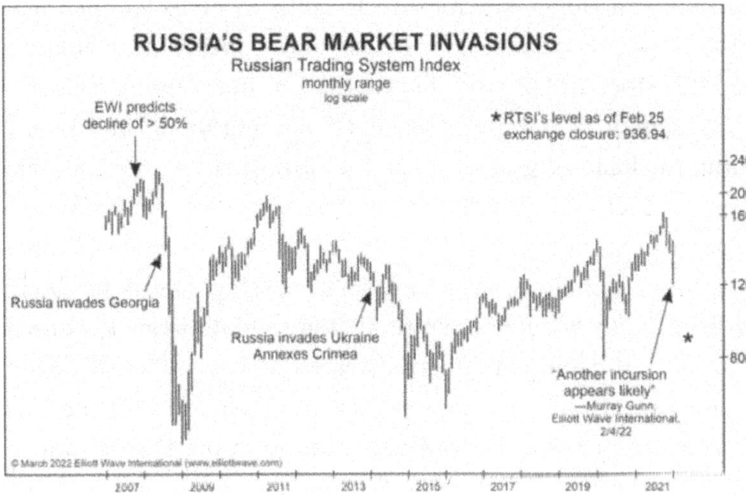

Chart 1. A prediction that the war would bottom out at a support range of 1000–800 points.

The background history of the pattern is as follows. Back in May 2008, Elliott Wave researcher, Alan Hall, had accurately predicted that the RTSI index would hit its zenith, foreshadowing a dramatic crash in market sentiment. As the stock index indeed plummeted by 79.9%, Russia escalated its geopolitical maneuvers by deploying troops into the contested Abkhazia region of Georgia. This aggressive move swiftly intensified tensions, culminating in a full-blown conflict between Georgia and Russia.

Similarly, on December 9, 2013, Robert Folsom, an associate researcher at the Socionomics Institute, issued a cautionary forecast regarding Russia's potential actions towards Ukraine. In a striking fulfillment of this prediction, by March 2014, Russia had occupied and annexed Crimea, flagrantly disregarding international condemnation. This occurred shortly after Ukraine's pro-Russian president, Yanukovych, was ousted under immense pressure from persistent protesters. Following these events, the crisis deepened in Ukraine's eastern regions of Luhansk and Donetsk, which declared themselves independent entities. As a conclusion, it is clear that significant declines in the RTSI stock index preceded Russia's military interventions.

Relying on this hypotheses and following the RTSI, Murray Gunn, the head of global research at Elliott Wave International (EWI), anticipated another potential incursion in 2022. The Moscow stock market had begun its descent from its October 2021 high, coinciding with Russia's massing of troops along the Ukrainian border. Despite all the denials from President Vladimir Putin and Foreign Minister Sergei Lavrov, the invasion of Ukraine began. On February 24, 2022, Russia launched its invasion of Ukraine, perfectly aligning with the RTSI's plunge below the critical 1000-point threshold[8] — exactly the same day! Since my book was just published on 24 January, and as I was interviewed on a podcast the same day, I got my own little moment to act as a prophet on the matter a month before the extreme event happened. When the attack started, I was startled — I noticed that my Twitter account had been closed. I had just posted my above-mentioned prediction and some other things from my book. A friend of mine who has taught cybersecurity at the university comforted me; "it's not about you, it's probably about military censorship — you have to be careful these days, after all there is a war going on."

So, how huge a role does social mood play in people's behavior?

It may have a much larger role in society than anyone currently realizes, I thought. But what is the social mood like? We'll figure it out in the next chapter.

8. A more detailed description of the analysis can be found in Ketovuori, M. (2024). *Socionomics: How Social Mood Shapes Society*. Routledge, London, pp. 105–109.

Chapter 4

The Essence and Phases of Mood

Moods should be heard but never danced to – **Hugh Prather**

For over a century, the field of psychology has largely operated under the premise of humans as inherently rational beings. However, let's consider this for a moment — what if this assumption is flawed? What if humans are not primarily rational creatures, but rather sentient beings driven also by emotions and instincts? This paradigm shift suggests that our understanding of human behavior could evolve from viewing individuals as isolated *Homo sapiens* to recognizing them as part of a more interconnected and empathetic members of the herd — *Homo sentiens*.

Imagine immersing yourself in the following moments, each with its own unique social undertones and emotional nuances. As you empathize and place yourself within these situations, consider the subtle waves of social mood that ebb and flow behind the scenes.

- A moment in a café: While entering a bustling city cafe, the aroma of freshly brewed coffee fills the air. A few moments after, as you sip your cappuccino, you notice the lively chatter of customers and staff around you — a mix of laughter, animated discussions, and the gentle clinking of cups. The cafe creates a strong feeling of community and connection, where people's interactions come together in a shared space. This is your first time here, will you come here again? The mood will decide that.
- Family reunion: Picture yourself at a family gathering, where generations come together under one roof. The warmth of familial bonds is almost tangible, as stories of the past are recounted with nostalgia and laughter.

Yet, amidst the joy, there are undercurrents of unspoken tensions and unresolved conflicts, subtly influencing the atmosphere. It reminds you of the complex layers that exist within even the most loving relationships. The preceding mood (or former experiences as you rationalize it) is already set, before arriving at the gathering.

- Walking in the park: You are having a nice, calm evening walk in a quiet park with a sunset sky. As you stroll, you see couples holding hands, children playing and laughing, and people lost in thought. The nature around you contrasts with the emotions and stories of those you pass. Each person adds life to the peaceful natural setting. How do you feel? Are you grateful, curious, or for some other reason, are your thoughts somewhere else? What is the mood of the park?

In each of these situations, the social mood acts as an invisible thread, subtly weaving through and influencing the interactions and emotions at play. Mood is, however, not the same thing than personal emotion, it is something longer lasting, underlying and socially shared. Now, envision the following scenarios as if you were present at these events.

- Police in danger: If a policeman is convinced that a man poses a threat to your life, and your survival instinct leads you to believe that a bullet is the only way to neutralize this threat, it appears rational to shoot him. However, rationalization can invert this process — he shoots the man first and then convinces himself that he posed a life-threatening danger.[9]
- One morning at the workplace: On a bright, crisp morning, you arrive at the office, feeling slightly flustered after a frustrating search for a parking spot. Normally, such tardiness would go unnoticed. However, today feels different. The usual office buzz is conspicuously absent:

no cheerful conversations, no ringing phones — just a heavy silence. Colleagues exchange furtive glances; some fixated on their screens. You hesitate before taking your seat, quietly observing the uneasy atmosphere. Suddenly, a notification appears on your monitor: *Company-wide emergency meeting in 10 minutes.* Your heart skips a beat. Clearly, something significant has happened, and it is about to reshape everything. Somehow, on the level of mood, you knew that this was coming.

- May 17, 2000, Copenhagen: The streets of Copenhagen were filled with anticipation as Arsenal and Galatasaray fans gathered for the UEFA Cup Final. However, past incidents involving Leeds United fans in Istanbul had already sowed seeds of tension. As night fell, what started as friendly interactions quickly turned sour, and a single thrown bottle ignited chaos. Fans clashed, and small scuffles escalated into full-blown riots. Flares lit up the sky as police struggled to regain control. By morning, the city bore the scars of the night's violence. What was intended to be a celebratory event had devolved into what came to be known as "the battle of Copenhagen." In the aftermath, four people were stabbed, nineteen were injured, and sixty were arrested. The mood drove the events.

In the first scenario, a police officer tries to justify his actions with logic, even though his behavior is mainly influenced by strong emotions and preceding mood. The instinctive, quick-thinking mind often acts faster than the logical mind, leading to situations like firing a weapon before fully understanding the consequences. Afterward, the officer's rational mind tries to piece together a story that makes the events look better. The mood, full of anxiety, fear, and stress, can lead to shooting incidents. These kind of situations are often discussed in police training sessions, but sometimes such incidents still occur.

In the second scenario, set against the backdrop of the workplace, we witness how rapidly and noticeably the mood can transform, with everyone instantly feeling the shift. Upon reflection, many individuals assert that they had a gut feeling about impending changes well before they actually transpired. Intriguingly, the mood within a workplace tends to remain enduring, as if *the social mood is embedded in the very walls of the place*, even as employees come and go. The social mood is a hidden force, exerting a profound influence on events in workplaces.

In the third real-life scenario, the Copenhagen riots serve as a prime example, fueled by a prolonged period of negative social mood, justified and rationalized by previous events in Istanbul. The rioters, acting in unison like a herd, were driven by a shared, burgeoning emotion. However, once detained, each individual was held responsible for their actions, despite the collective nature of his or her behavior. In today's advanced technological landscape, the mood of a sports audience can be accurately forecast through the integration of a sophisticated camera surveillance system and cutting-edge artificial intelligence. By analyzing a substantial volume of facial expressions, this system can identify a predominance of negative emotions, effectively predicting potential unrest or dissatisfaction following a match.

Despite the lucidity of the previous scenarios, it is truly remarkable how seldom social mood is acknowledged. The lack of attention isn't just due to a shortage of academic research or literature; it's also a reflection of how dominant worldviews dictate our thinking. Modern thought, particularly in economics and social sciences, tends to emphasize rationality and linear cause-and-effect reasoning. This perspective underestimates the role of emotions, crowd psychology, and subconscious collective sentiment in shaping events and society. However, there are also purely practical reasons why so many people don't notice social mood. If social mood is endogenous, meaning it arises within society rather than being triggered by external events, it is difficult to detect. If it is also unconscious, something that people feel but don't explicitly think about, you don't notice it; and because it is unremembered, it also passes without leaving a clear trace in memory.

Despite all this, social mood is constantly present, and everyone is susceptible to it, whether we notice it or not. This all, of course, fits with the idea that social mood is more of a background force that shapes attitudes and behavior and thus implicitly shapes society. However, when people recognize a change in mood, they often elaborate rational explanations afterwards, that fit the narrative, rather than acknowledging the organic and subconscious nature of the change. The difference between exogenous (event-driven moods) and endogenous (mood-driven events) thinking can be tested using the following examples.

Table 2. **Mechanical vs. socionomic causality (Prechter 2016, 119).**

Mechanical causality (exogeneous cause)	**Socionomic causality (endogenous cause)**
Social events determine the tenor and character of social mood	**Social mood determines the tenor and character of social events.**
Recession causes businesspeople to be cautious.	Cautious businesspeople cause recession.
Talented leaders make the population happy.	A happy population makes leaders appear talented.
A rising stock market makes people increasingly optimistic.	Increasingly optimistic people make the stock market rise.
Scandals make people outraged.	Outraged people seek out scandals
The availability of derivates fosters a desire to speculate.	A desire to speculate fosters the availability of derivates.

(Continued)

War makes people fearful and angry.	A fearful and angry people make war.
Epidemics cause society to be fearful and depressed.	A depressed and fearful society is susceptible to epidemics.
Happy music makes people smile.	People who want to smile choose happy music.
Nuclear bomb testing makes people nervous.	Nervous people test nuclear bombs.
The success of financial television spurred excitement among investors.	Excited investors spurred the success of financial television.
An expanding economy puts people in a good mood.	People in a good mood generate an expanding economy.
Falling markets make investors fearful.	Fearful investors make markets fall.
Good news makes stock rise, and bad news make them fall.	No, it doesn't. They just coincide sometimes.

When assessing the scenarios outlined above, the question to consider is which scenarios hold greater plausibility? For example, using an example from the table to evaluate "happy music makes people smile" versus "people who want to smile choose happy music," which one is true? According to Prechter, those who desire to smile are naturally drawn to happy music. While it is also true that happy music has the potential to uplift those feeling down, the music people select is, however, predominantly influenced by the prevailing social mood (rather than their personal choices).

Taking another example from the table, the distinction between the argumentative sentences "Scandals make people outraged" and "outraged people seek scandals" lies in the direction of causality and the resulting implications. The first sentence suggests that scandals are the initial trigger, causing people to become outraged. In this scenario, the focus is on the impact of scandals, acting as a catalyst for public emotion and reaction. The second sentence, however, suggests that people who are already angry look for scandals to confirm their feelings or to have a place to express their dissatisfaction. This shows that these individuals actively seek out confrontation. In today's society, it is well known that being judgmental and the eagerness to search for scandals have become more common as an almost established way of dealing with things and other people.

As a third example, consider the contrasting statements: "Talented leaders make the population happy" versus "A happy population makes leaders appear talented." These sentences prompt a debate about the true source of leadership. Do skilled leaders naturally increase the well-being and satisfaction of their citizens, or does a satisfied and prosperous population increase the perceived abilities of their leaders?

While more recent examples might be available to illustrate this idea, President Ronald Reagan's tenure is a great example in this regard. Was Reagan simply a fortunate politician or indeed a gifted leader; or perhaps, a combination of both? While his presidency was marked by an era of optimism, his charismatic character certainly played a great role in the economic recovery following the crippling stagflation of the 1970s. Under Reagan's leadership, a change in the nation's mood and economy occurred. However, the philosophical question is whether the nation chose a leader that resonated with the era, or did Ronald Reagan's exceptional talents truly transform the mood of the nation? What about the POTUS, what is the mood of the nation now compared to the 1980s? At least the presidents share the same slogan: *Let's Make America Great Again*. The question remains: do they share the same mood?

Picture 1. Presidential portraits of two presidents of the United States of America

The potential explanation of Reagan's popularity mirrors Prechter's analysis of the popularity of the Beatles. According to the study:

> *achieving phenomenal status necessitates ambition, favorable circumstances, and impeccable timing. Nonetheless, once a breakthrough is made, a band's popularity is largely dictated by the prevailing social mood. Thus, performing artists cannot generate happiness within society; they can only reflect and symbolize it.*[10]

Similarly, it is likely that Ronald Reagan's ascent to the presidency was not solely due to his personal charm and character but was significantly influenced by the social mood of his era.

Nations tend to choose leaders who resonate with their collective emotional state rather than based on their abilities. For this reason, it is essential to understand that leaders do not shape their times or create their mood, but instead we should analyze the social mood of the nation and the values and attitudes that emerge from it.

The essence of social mood is deeply intertwined with the flow of time, permeating beyond fleeting instants to influence every facet of life. This collective emotional tapestry imbues our interactions with color, shapes, societal norms, sways of political decisions, and sculpts entire cultures, mirroring the vibrant and ever-evolving mosaic of human experience. The pervasive impact of social mood is evident across various fields, from the design of architecture to the hues of automobiles, the trends in fashion to the themes explored in cinema. The narrow-minded rational mind does not see these colors of life and is therefore incapable of understanding it. It is not surprising that despite their intellectual prowess, many scientists remain largely oblivious to the concept of mood. Evidence supporting this idea is often hastily dismissed as mere speculation, without the consideration it merits. Fair enough! Let's look at the phases of social mood, as already presented in the chapter one.

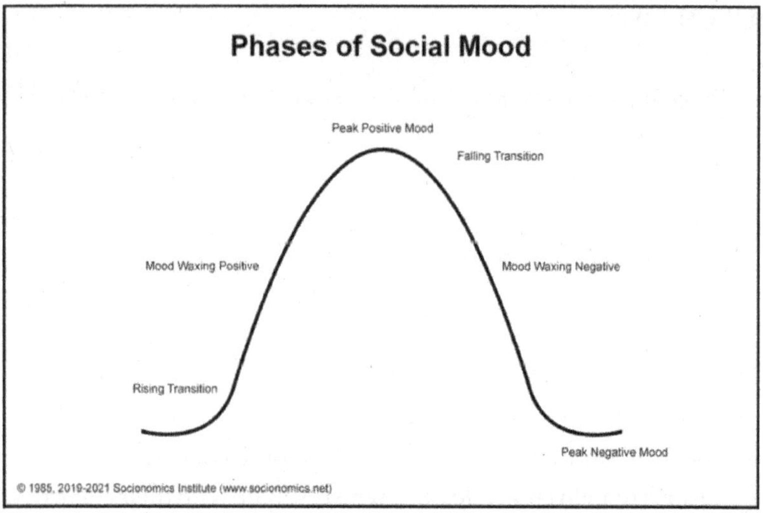

Figure 6. Phases of social mood

The four phases of social mood with corresponding emotions are:

1. Mood Rising (hope) — Society is becoming more optimistic. People are hopeful about the future, economic activity picks up, and cultural trends reflect positivity.
2. Mood Peak (hubris) — Optimism is at its highest. Stock markets boom, innovation thrives, and confidence is widespread. However, this often leads to overconfidence and bubbles.
3. Mood Declining (fear) — Pessimism starts creeping in. Economic slowdowns, social tensions, and distrust in institutions increase. Negative cultural trends emerge.
4. Mood Bottom (despair) — Pessimism is at its worst. Financial crises, conflicts, and cultural stagnation dominate. However, this phase often sets the stage for a new rise in optimism.

Measuring the waves involves tracking financial, cultural, and psychological indicators as well as stock market trends, consumer confidence, and corporate investments. Social trends, such as shifts in popular media, fashion, and crime rates, reflect collective mood, as additionally, sentiment analysis of news and social media helps gauge the public's mood in real-time. By combining all these indicators, analysts can better understand society's emotional state and anticipate major economic and cultural shifts. Recognizing these patterns can help individuals, businesses, and policymakers navigate changing times and anticipate the future, as these social mood cycles repeat over time, shaping history and societies. Sociometrics can be summarized in the mathematization of measurable phenomena and the measurement of meaningful differences in change.

Perhaps the most widely known sociometer is the skyscraper index,[11] explored by Andrew Lawrence in 1999, that suggests a link between the construction of the world's tallest buildings and impending economic downturns or depressions. This theory posits that the completion of record-setting skyscrapers often coincides with, or precedes, economic busts. The underlying idea is that these architectural giants are typically built during periods of excessive economic optimism and speculative investment, which then lead to overextension and eventual market corrections. Historically, this pattern has been observed with structures like the Empire State Building, the World Trade Center, and the Burj Khalifa, all of which were completed around the time of significant financial upheavals.

The predictive power of the Skyscraper Index is undeniable, while Lawrence's observations cover a period of over a hundred years. For instance, the Panic of 1907 was preceded by the construction of the Singer Building and the Metropolitan Life Building, completed in 1908 and 1909, respectively. Similarly, the Great Depression was foreshadowed by the completion of monumental structures like 40 Wall Tower in 1929, the Chrysler Building in 1930, and the Empire State Building in 1931. The last one had a nickname, "an empire empty building" during the 1930s, as no-one needed office space at that time. Similarly, the Sears Tower and the World Trade Center were nearing completion in 1973, coinciding with the onset of the oil crisis that plunged global markets into chaos. The Petronas Towers rose in 1998 amidst the Asian Financial Crisis, and the Burj Khalifa, the tallest building to date, was completed in 2010, shortly after the 2008 Global Financial Crisis had wreaked havoc worldwide.

Just as a thermometer is not designed to measure wind speed, even though wind can significantly influence how temperature is felt, the skyscraper sociometer is adept at predicting major shifts in the economy. Lawrence's research reveals that the inception of these monumental skyscraper projects typically occurs during the later phases of an economic boom, characterized by robust growth and low unemployment rates. These times of heightened optimism are often succeeded by significant financial corrections, economic recessions, or even depressions, which are marked by increasing unemployment. Interestingly, skyscrapers frequently

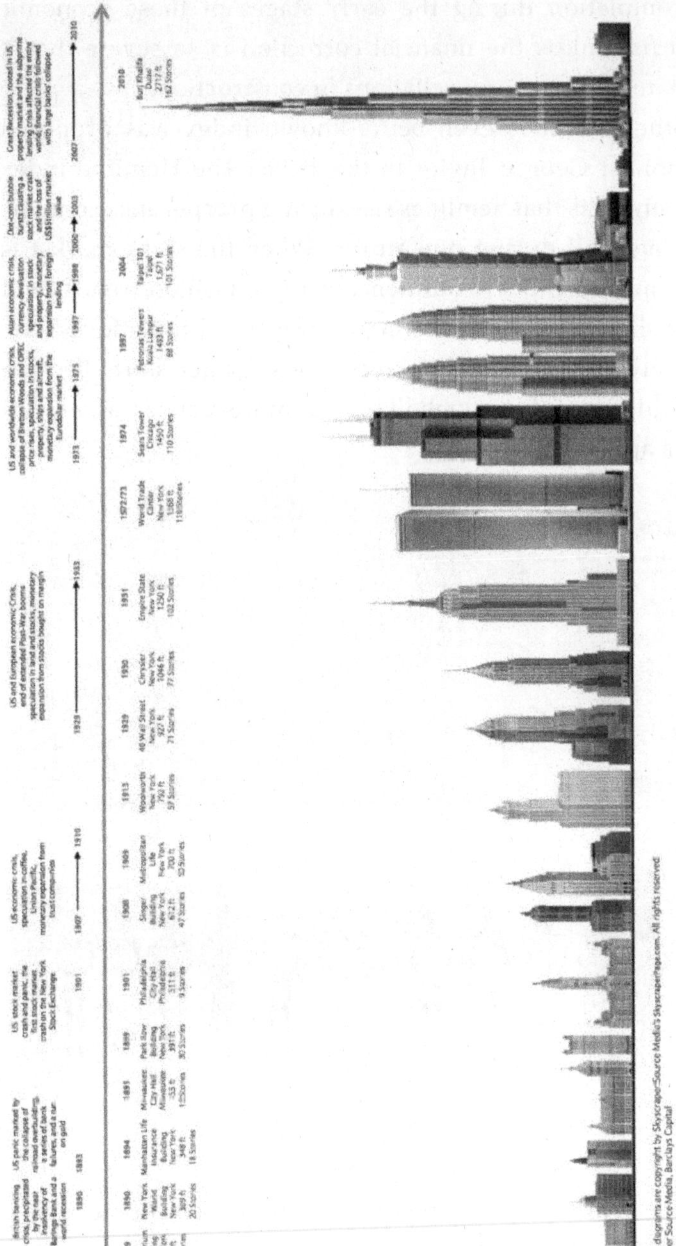

Picture 2. Skyscraper Index

reach completion during the early stages of these economic downturns, unless the financial correction is so severe that it necessitates delays or cancellations in construction.

Another, perhaps even better-known index was proposed by economist George Taylor in the 1920s. The Hemline Index Theory suggests that hemlines rise during prosperous economic periods and fall during downturns. When the stock market is thriving and consumer confidence is high, fashion trends tend to favor shorter skirts, reflecting a carefree, optimistic society. Conversely, during economic recessions, longer skirts become fashionable, possibly symbolizing a more conservative and cautious approach.

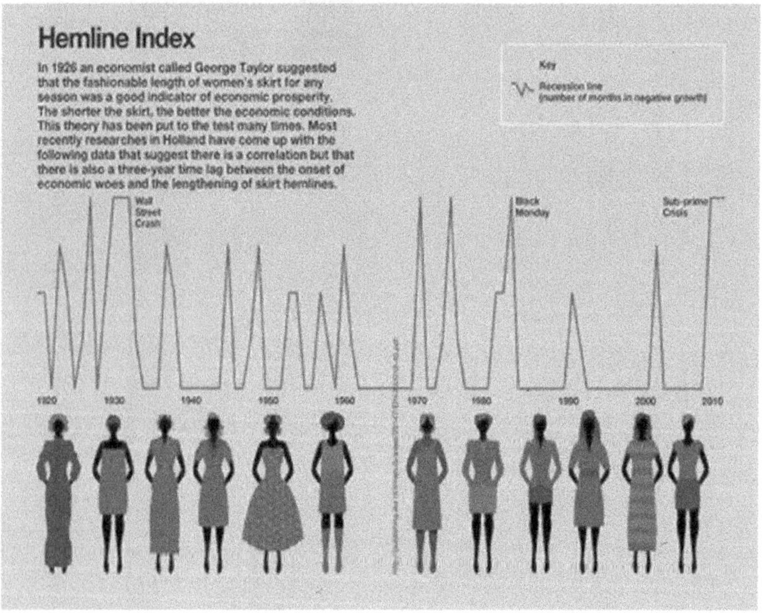

Picture 3. Hemline index

Over the years, Taylor's theory has been reevaluated and, generally speaking, its observations still hold validity.[12] Although not without its critics, the theory continues to serve as an interesting lens through which to examine the intersection of economics and fashion. While measuring the height of the world's tallest skyscrapers might be a straightforward task, attempting to gauge the length of every woman's skirt at a given moment is practically impossible. However, the drive for generalization through statistical accuracy is a hallmark of engineering thinking. This pursuit highlights at least two significant limitations: a lack of understanding of cultural nuances and an inability to interpret qualitative aspects. A logical explanation underpins this approach: criticism of sociometric indicators is rooted in the principle that correlation does not imply causation. In traditional scientific thought, correlation alone cannot substantiate a connection between phenomena and thus cannot claim truth.

In the realm of skyscrapers, the relationship between financial speculation and the enthusiasm for construction is undoubtedly interconnected. However, there is no direct causal link; rather, the underlying connection is the peak of a positive social mood. Although the extent of overinvestment and the height of the rising buildings can be measured, these are manifestations of social mood, which itself can only be approached through external features, and as such, cannot be proven true or false in the traditional sense. However, the inability to quantify something precisely, does not negate its existence or significance.

To sum it up – although we cannot define the nature of social mood exhaustively, it possesses the following characteristics:

- Social mood is influenced by a natural herding instinct found in human behavior.
- This instinct encourages individuals within a society to synchronize with the prevailing social mood, thereby shaping collective behaviors and attitudes.
- These collective behaviors then manifest as societal events and phenomena.

The essence of social mood can be encapsulated in the following three principles:

- Social mood is always present in society.
- Social mood does not depend on external factors.
- Social mood does not directly dictate the events; it only shapes them.

Over the course of more than twenty years dedicated to the exploration of this subject, I have gained a deep appreciation for the intricate and multifaceted nature of social mood. This concept is not only elusive but also complex, encompassing a vast array of variables and influences that render its study both challenging and captivating.

In exploring the quintessence of social mood, it is imperative to consider its historical significance, where its impact has been remarkably evident. By scrutinizing how social mood has shaped pivotal historical events and propelled cultural transformations, we can uncover invaluable insights into its role throughout history. Furthermore, there exist specific locations where ephemeral and localized moods are transmitted and transcend into universal and historical significance.

9. Cushman (2020). Interestingly the article called "Rationalization is rational" is lacking the role of emotions, not to mention that of mood, completely!
10. Prechter, R. R. (2017). *Socionomic Studies of Society and Culture.* Socionomics Institute Press, pp. 3–56.
11. Thorton, Mark (2005). "Skyscrapers and Business Cycles," *Quarterly Journal of Austrian Economics 8*: pp. 51–74.
12. Van Baardwijk, M., and Franses, P. H. (2010). "The hemline and the economy: is there any match?" *Report / Econometric Institute, Erasmus University Rotterdam,* pp. 1–11.

Chapter 5

At the Highgate Cemetery

No one here gets out alive.

– Jim Morrison

As the sun rises over Highgate Cemetery in North London casting its golden light across weathered tombstones, the silence is broken only by the whispers of history – or perhaps it is the gentle sound of rain dripping from the trees. Highgate is more than just a burial ground, this hallowed site is a reflection of societal change, a place where the past lingers and where, perhaps, the future can be glimpsed in its silent monuments.

Reaching Highgate Cemetery from central London is a journey in itself, one that winds through the city's historic heart. The Northern Line of the London Underground carries visitors to Archway Station, where the climb up Highgate Hill offers a glimpse of charming streets and centuries-old architecture. Alternatively, buses such as the 210 weave their way to Highgate Village, from which the cemetery lies just a short walk away. Upon arrival, visitors are required to pay an entrance fee – a small price for stepping into a world where history and nature are entwined. The cemetery is divided into two sections: the East and the West.

The West Cemetery is a masterpiece of Victorian Gothic design, home to the dramatic Egyptian Avenue and the breathtaking Circle of Lebanon. The East Cemetery is the final resting place of a diverse array of figures, including some from contemporary history whose names still echo in modern headlines, such as Karl Marx, George Eliot, Douglas Adams, and Malcolm McLaren. In the West Cemetery lies also

Alexander Litvinenko, the former Russian spy who died in 2006 after being poisoned with Polonium-210, dropped into his green tea at the Pine Bar of Hotel Millenium, Mayfair.[13] His death, orchestrated with a substance so rare and lethal that its estimated black-market value reached ten million dollars per gram, underscored the sinister reach of geopolitical intrigue. Though the poison originated from a state-controlled facility near Yekaterinburg, its cost remains a theoretical concern in a case that continues to haunt international relations. Addressing his final words to Vladimir Putin from his deathbed, Litvinenko directly accused the Russian leader of orchestrating his assassination.

While Russians officials vehemently denied any involvement, dismissing the claims as anti-Russian propaganda, state-controlled media portrayed Litvinenko as a traitor and defector whose death was being exploited to tarnish Russia's reputation. The Kremlin labelled the accusations absurd, while Russian diplomats accused Britain of using the case to fuel political tensions. However, Western investigations, including a UK public inquiry in 2016,[14] concluded that Litvinenko was likely poisoned by FSB agents Andrei Lugovoi and Dmitry Kovtun, acting "probably under the direction" of the Russian state – deepening the divide between Moscow and the West. As a haunting reminder of the dangerous intersection between politics espionage, and betrayal, his image is found at the floor of the tombstone.

Picture 4. Alexander Litvinenko (1962–2006)

Despite the rich history and the many notable graves scattered throughout the cemetery, most visitors come to Highgate cemetery primarily to pay their respects to Karl Marx. Marx's critical analysis of capitalism and his advocacy for a classless society seem to continue to resonate with many. Tourists and admirers gather at his grave, taking photographs, leaving flowers, and sometimes even singing *The Internationale*. The site has become some sort of a pilgrimage for his followers, where they unite in solidarity. Yet, as they do, I can't help but wonder if they notice the silent witness behind them, namely Herbert Spencer, resting diagonally opposite on the other side of the path just a few yards from his colleague.

The resting places of Herbert Spencer and Karl Marx in Highgate Cemetery serve as a symbolic contrast between two vastly different worldviews — one rooted in optimism, the other in struggle. Spencer, the champion of social Darwinism and free-market capitalism, saw society as an evolving organism where competition and self-improvement would lead to progress. He believed that human advancement was a natural process, driven by individual effort rather than state intervention. His optimism aligned with the expansion of industrial capitalism, particularly during times of economic prosperity, when societies embraced liberalism, deregulation, and technological progress. This Spencerian optimism was later reflected in periods of strong social mood, such as the neoliberal wave of the 1980s, when Reagan and Thatcher revived free-market policies, echoing Spencer's belief in the survival of the economically fittest.

In stark contrast, Karl Marx embodied the struggle of the working class, viewing history as a battleground of economic oppression. Witnessing the brutal realities of early capitalism, Marx saw inequality and exploitation as defining features of the system, which he believed would inevitably collapse through revolution. Unlike Spencer's faith in natural progress, Marx argued that class conflict was inescapable, requiring a radical restructuring of society. His pessimism found resonance during periods of economic crisis, such as the Great Depression, when faith in free markets crumbled, and governments embraced interventionist policies, moving closer to Marxist principles. Even in postwar Europe, elements of Marxist thought shaped the creation of social welfare states, challenging Spencer's vision of minimal government. Despite his pessimism, Marx's ideas continued to fuel revolutionary movements, including the rise of Soviet communism, though history ultimately exposed the flaws in centrally planned economies.

The shifting tides of social mood — between optimism and despair, free markets and state control — have dictated which thinker's ideas gain influence at different times. Spencer's *laissez-faire* optimism flourished in times of economic expansion, while Marx's calls for revolution gains traction during downturns. In

Picture 5. The tombs of Karl Marx (1818–1883) and Herbert Spencer (1820–1903)

life, they stood on opposite ends of the ideological spectrum — in death, they now share peace, equality, and perhaps shared conversations in a peaceful environment? Of course, after the tourists have left the area leaving space for quiet discussion...

In his lifetime, Marx might have relished the chance to debate Spencer in person. Despite living in London at the same time, and knowing each other's ideas, the two never met. As Marx's English was not quite fluent enough for complex discussion, their vastly different social circles made an encounter highly unlikely. Spencer, a member of the exclusive *Athenaeum Club*, moved among London's intellectual elite, discussing ideas with scientists, politicians, and writers, while Marx, often living in financial hardship, relied on the generosity of his friend, Friedrich Engels, spending his days in the reading room of the British Museum rather than in the company of aristocratic thinkers.

Yet one cannot help but wonder, what if they had met? Could their debate have shaped a different trajectory for history, one in which revolution and capitalism found some unlikely reconciliation? Perhaps the discussion would have progressed, according to the rules of dialectics, from thesis through antithesis to the synthesis, such as:

Marx: "The workers must control the means of production!"
Spencer: "Nonsense! Progress comes from competition and individual enterprise!"
Marx: "So you propose a society where goods are exchanged freely, yet the workers still have a stake?"
Spencer: "Exactly! A system where quality determines success, and people are free to choose!"
Marx: *pauses* "You know, that almost sounds... fair."
Spencer: "It does, doesn't it? Perhaps we should put our names on it."
Marx: *stroking his beard* "Marx and Spencer?"
Spencer: "Now that's a business I could believe in!"

And so, instead of sparking revolutions, the two would have revolutionized retail, offering affordable quality to all. Who knows — at least the year that the store chain was founded fits the pattern well. Since Marx died in 1883, it must be Spencer, who eventually carried out their common plan.

M&S
EST. 1884

Picture 6. M&S Logo

Perhaps this is the greatest lesson of Highgate: even the most drastic divisions in the living world fade with time, leaving behind only thoughts, memories, and the silent witnesses of history. The social mood behind the memories, however, continues to shape the world as it did during the times of Marx and Spencer. Well, the truth is, we don't know what the truth is … yet, too often, people try to force reality to conform to their ideas rather than letting their ideas be shaped by reality.

And unfortunately, they do not stop there as dogmatic beliefs are rarely kept to oneself. Instead, they are imposed on others, whether through persuasion, coercion, or outright censorship (or poisoning someone with Polonium-210). Why? Because uncertainty is uncomfortable, and those who claim absolute truth often try to silence dissent to maintain their own sense of control. In the next chapter, we will explore how this battle plays out in the realms of freedom and censorship.

13. Harding, Luke (2016). *A Very Expensive Poison.* Guardian Books, London.
14. https://assets.publishing.service.gov.uk/media/5a803439e5274a2e8ab4eca4/The-Litvinenko-Inquiry-H-C-695.pdf

Chapter 6

Freedom Versus Control

If liberty means anything at all, it means the right to tell people things they do not want to hear.

– **George Orwell**

In Finland, when an individual successfully defends a doctoral dissertation, it is customary to host a celebration known as a "karonkka." This elegant gathering is traditionally organized to honor the opponents who evaluated the thesis, though it is a well-known fact that the spotlight truly shines on the newly conferred doctor. The guest list typically includes the doctoral candidate's family, friends, and colleagues from the university. Given Finland's rich cultural heritage and adherence to tradition, attendees of the karonkka don formal attire, with men in tailcoats and women in elegant evening dresses.

The evening is marked by a series of ceremonial toasts and responses, and a formal dinner is typically served, accompanied by performances such as choir singing, enhancing the festive and sophisticated ambiance. It is also customary for the newly minted doctor to receive congratulatory gifts from attendees, which often include significant and thoughtful items. I myself received a remarkable collection of books as a gift, in the form of the collected works of Aristotle and Plato, as well as a particularly fascinating collection of fiction – a box of forbidden books by Penguin containing 12 famous books, following the order in the picture from top left to right down:

- Aleksandr Solzhenitsyn: *One Day in the Life of Ivan Denisovich* – this book, set in a Soviet labor camp, was banned in the USSR for its critical portrayal of the regime.

- George Orwell: *Animal Farm* – banned in the USSR due to its anti-communist themes.
- John Steinbeck: *Of Mice and Men* – faced censorship in the US for perceived obscenity and controversial political themes.
- Anthony Burgess: *A Clockwork Orange* – banned in the US for social obscenity and its depiction of violence.
- Federico García Lorca: *Poet in New York* – censored in Spain during the Franco regime due to its radical political content.
- Chinua Achebe: *Things Fall Apart* – banned in Kenya and the Congo for alleged obscenity.

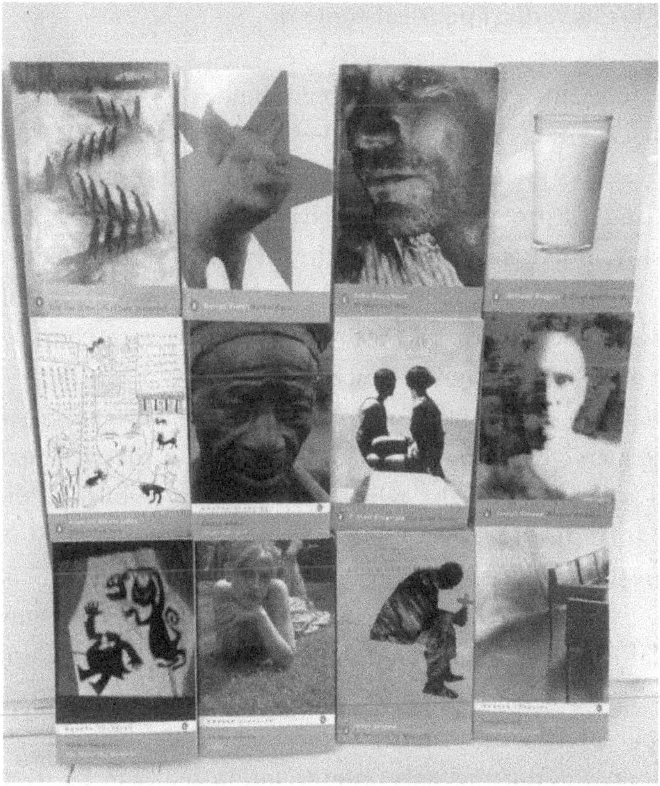

Picture 7. Collection of banned books

- F. Scott Fitzgerald: *The Great Gatsby* – banned in the US for obscenity.
- Joseph Conrad: *Heart of Darkness* – banned for political reasons in Poland, Germany, and the USSR.
- Mikhail Bulgakov: *The Master and Margarita* – banned in the USSR for its radical political implications. Bulgakov had a complex relationship with Stalin, admiring him yet fearing his wrath.
- Vladimir Nabokov: *Lolita* – banned in France, Argentina, and New Zealand due to its controversial themes of obscenity.
- James Baldwin: *Go Tell It on the Mountain* – censored in the US for social obscenity.
- George Orwell: *Nineteen Eighty-Four* – banned in Cuba for its radical political content.

From this collection, I have read both of Orwell's works, Steinbeck, Fitzgerald, and Bulgakov's *The Master and Margarita*. In Bulgakov's novel, Voland, a mysterious and enigmatic figure disguised as a professor, is revealed to be Satan himself, engaging in a surreal and supernatural narrative. The story intertwines with Walpurgis Night and travels back to Jerusalem, featuring Pontius Pilate and Jesus (Yeshua Ha-Notsri) in a captivating court drama. Although this scene is important it still is only one of many, as the story unfolds across a tapestry of diverse and immersive settings, each contributing to the rich texture of the tale. Interestingly, while the book was published under its original title *The Master and Margarita* in English, in Finland the novel was released in 1969 under the intriguing title *Saatana saapuu Moskovaan* "Satan arrives to Moscow." The Finnish translator's interpretation highlighted the book's exploration of the surreal and often bizarre aspects of Soviet society. This perspective is certainly supported by the original story, although it is not the only interpretation that can be derived from Bulgakov's complex narrative.

Mikhail Bulgakov, a writer who both revered and dreaded Joseph Stalin, skillfully navigated the oppressive waters of censorship while maintaining his artistic liberty. His brilliance shines through in his ability to weave a narrative that invites readers to ponder: Has Satan ever truly vacated the city after making his ominous entrance?

The enigmatic nature of Bulgakov's genius style not only serves as a commentary on the political climate of his time but also invites the audience to reflect on the persistent presence of evil and chaos in society. This timeless exploration is precisely what imbues the novel with its enduring appeal, as every interpretation holds validity and is open to new interpretations. This leads us to consider a broader context where literature grapples with the boundaries of freedom and expression.

There is an inherent irony in the fact that a writer must fear the consequences of his own creation. This fear stems from the potential political, social, or personal consequences of challenging the status quo or offending those in power. Throughout history, literature has been continually suppressed, confirming that books have the power to provoke, shock, and threaten authority. The ups and downs between times of censorship and times of freedom have reflected the prevailing social mood. In negative times, censorship increases and clamps down on free speech, while in positive times, restrictions are loosened. Whether it is state-imposed bans, religious restrictions, or ideological blacklists, the suppression of literature reflects the ongoing struggle between control and free expression, which is a testament to the enduring power of the written word.

In Ancient Rome, the *censor*, a magistrate whose role was to "monitor morality," was responsible for conducting the census and overseeing public behavior. Centuries later, the Catholic Church institutionalized censorship in 1559 through the *Index Librorum Prohibitorum*, a list of forbidden books deemed dangerous to faith and morals. This index, which remained in use until 1966, banned works considered heretical, impure, or subversive, including those by renowned writers such as Gustave Flaubert, Émile Zola, George Sand, and Simone de Beauvoir.[15]

In the Soviet Union, spanning from the 1920s to the 1990s, censorship was a crucial mechanism for the regime to exert control over intellectual and cultural life. The state imposed strict regulations on literature, media, and the arts, targeting any material deemed critical of the government or misaligned with socialist principles. Intellectuals, writers, and artists who resisted faced severe repercussions, including imprisonment, exile, or even execution. Notable figures such as Boris Pasternak and Aleksandr Solzhenitsyn, whose works unveiled the harsh realities of Soviet life, endured significant penalties for their dissent. This censorship not only targeted politically sensitive content but also aimed to stifle any artistic expression that diverged from the prescribed Soviet narrative.

Similarly, during the Cultural Revolution in China (1966–1976), Chairman Mao Zedong's regime enforced stringent censorship to eradicate what it perceived as "counterrevolutionary" elements. Traditional books, art, and cultural artifacts, especially those with Western influences, were destroyed. This era was marked by the persecution of intellectuals, many of whom were sent to labor camps or publicly humiliated. Mao's government prioritized promoting his writings and ideas, silencing any dissenting voices. This period of censorship significantly impacted Chinese culture and education, as it attempted to obliterate any intellectual or artistic expression that did not align with Maoist ideology.

China and the former USSR are easy targets for criticism, but they are not alone in their history of suppressing dissenting voices. The United States, too, has faced its own dark chapter of silencing dissents during the Cold War era, specifically during the period known as McCarthyism (1940s to 1950s). Spearheaded by Senator Joseph McCarthy, this fervent anti-communist crusade sought to eradicate supposed communist influence throughout the nation. This campaign resulted in the blacklisting of numerous individuals across various sectors including entertainment, government, and academia. Esteemed artists, writers, and intellectuals found their careers and reputations in tatters, often based on mere allegations of communist ties. One of the most prominent figures affected was the legendary Charlie Chaplin. Despite his immense contributions to the film industry, Chaplin was compelled to leave the United States and seek asylum in Europe due to the intense scrutiny and suspicion he faced during this period. While history has often judged such moments as cautionary tales of overreach and repression, echoes of similar situations still happen today.

In recent years, the United States has witnessed a significant increase in book censorship, particularly within public schools and libraries. The 2023–2024 school year witnessed an alarming surge in book bans, reaching nearly 10,000, which represents a staggering 200 percent increase from the previous year.[16] This dramatic rise highlights the paradox of a contemporary society that increasingly censors diverse voices and ideas, despite the foundational principles of free speech laid by visionary thinkers who valued open dialogue for human progress:

- John Stuart Mill, in his influential work *On Liberty* (1859), warned against "the peculiar evil of silencing the expression of an opinion." He argued that such suppression robs humanity of not only current truths but also the chance to correct errors.
- Thomas Paine (1737–1809), a passionate advocate of individual rights, understood that the survival of democracy depended on the unfettered exchange of ideas. His pamphlet *Common Sense* (1776) ignited revolutionary sentiment, while *Rights of Man* (1791) defended the

freedoms that would later be enshrined in the First Amendment to the US Constitution (1791).
- James Madison (1751–1836), the principal architect of this amendment, ensured that freedom of speech would be a cornerstone of American democracy.

For over two centuries, this right has withstood war, political repression, and societal upheaval. But today, as communication shifts from printed pamphlets and public debates to rapid-fire digital discourse, the question remains: will these foundational ideals continue to hold firm? The battleground of free speech has moved from town squares and newspapers to the vast and fragmented world of the Internet. In an age where fewer people engage deeply with long-form literature, censorship remains a pressing issue, though it now manifests in new ways.

Instead of pamphlets like Paine's, political and ideological debates unfold in viral tweets, algorithm-driven feeds, and online echo chambers. The challenge today is not just government restriction but the influence of corporate platforms, artificial intelligence, and digital gatekeepers shaping what can and cannot be said. Understanding this shift is crucial, as it reflects not just technological change but the evolving tides of social mood — demanding, now more than ever, both historical awareness and patient engagement from those who seek to defend free expression.

In the realm of computing, this battle has evolved from playful hacker pranks in the 1970s to AI-driven censorship in the twenty-first century. What once began as irreverent experiments by early computer enthusiasts — such as changing system messages for amusement — has transformed into a sophisticated form of language policing that dictates what can and cannot be said on digital platforms. Today, artificial intelligence plays the role of the ultimate gatekeeper, filtering speech, shaping discourse, and enforcing ideological norms at an unprecedented scale.

In the early days of computing, particularly within institutions like MIT and Bell Labs, hacker culture was defined by a mix of intellectual elitism, irreverence, and playful rebellion. Hackers would modify system messages and implement "word bans" not out of ideological motives but as inside jokes or acts of defiance against bureaucratic oversight. The legendary prank of changing "users" to "losers" in computer labs was an example of this early word manipulation. It was a way for insiders to mock outsiders and exert control over the system.

However, as computers became more integrated into everyday life, the power to control language extended beyond hacker subcultures into the hands of corporations and institutions. What was once a game of linguistic subversion turned into a mechanism for enforcing social norms and controlling public discourse. With the expansion of social media and the mass digitization of communication, companies like Google, Facebook, X (Twitter), and YouTube began employing AI-driven moderation tools to filter content at scale. These algorithms were originally designed to combat spam and explicit material but have since been modified to control changing societal norms.

AI-driven censorship operates in various ways: detecting and removing content based on pre-flagged words, reducing the visibility of controversial opinions through algorithmic suppression, and embedding biases within training data that subtly reshape digital history. A notable example of this occurred during the COVID-19 pandemic, when Facebook and Twitter aggressively censored discussions questioning official health policies, some of which later turned out to be valid concerns. Users who shared alternative perspectives on lockdowns, vaccine efficacy, or the origins of the virus often found their posts removed or their accounts restricted.

These actions, though framed as misinformation control, inadvertently stifled open scientific discourse — an issue eerily reminiscent of Orwellian thought control, where only state-approved truths are permitted. This phenomenon has been extensively analyzed by scholars such as Shoshana Zuboff in (2019) *The Age of Surveillance Capitalism,* which explores how digital platforms have transformed into mechanisms of behavioral control.

However, the phenomenon of algorithmic censorship is not confined to one ideological side. While left-leaning institutions use AI to enforce progressive norms, such as banning words considered offensive or outdated, right-wing movements have responded with their own word restrictions, attempting to outlaw terms they do not like, such as "Latinx" or "climate change" in state documents. This development has created a feedback loop where both sides seek to dictate acceptable speech through technology, mirroring the historical battles over linguistic control in authoritarian regimes. The concerns over centralized control of speech echo — once again — the warnings of George Orwell's *Nineteen Eighty-Four,* where "Newspeak" was designed to limit the scope of thought itself. Beyond social media, AI censorship is extending into finance, governance, and even legal systems. Platforms like PayPal and Patreon have begun using AI to freeze accounts associated with speech they deem "misinformation" or "hate."

Predictive policing algorithms, originally designed to flag potential criminal behavior, have been applied to online speech, raising concerns about AI-driven pre-emptive censorship. Search engine manipulation subtly erases certain narratives from public discourse without outright banning them, influencing the flow of information in ways that are often invisible to users. The research of Eli Pariser on the "filter bubble" effect highlights how algorithmic personalization creates an environment where individuals are subtly guided away from conflicting viewpoints, reinforcing ideological silos.[17] As AI-driven censorship becomes more sophisticated, the implications for free expression are profound. The ability to shape language in real-time, suppress dissenting views, and promote officially sanctioned narratives represents an unprecedented level of control over human thought. The parallels to Orwell's work are striking – where technology does not just police work, but ultimately shapes what people believe to be true.

Yet, an even more unsettling question emerges: is AI changing human behavior to the point that we are becoming more like machines? Whereas early hacker culture thrived on creativity, defiance, and free-thinking, today's AI-driven world encourages conformity and self-censorship. It seems that AI is not just a tool for shaping discourse, but for conditioning human behavior itself. If AI is now evolving to become more human – learning language, detecting emotions, and predicting behavior – perhaps the real concern is that humans are becoming more like machines?

As the connection between digital technology and mental health has already become undeniable,[18] I am afraid we have not yet seen all its effect on humanity. If the social mood trend continues to decline towards despair, we will likely see social unrest and, once again, possibly persecution of various groups of people. This has always been the case and will continue to be the case. There are many historical examples of this.

Heinrich Heine's famous warning "Dort, wo man Bücher verbrennt, verbrennt man am Ende auch Menschen" was written in 1821 in his play *Almansor*. It referred to the destruction of the Quran by Christian forces during the Spanish Inquisition. Heine, a German-Jewish poet and intellectual, foresaw that censorship and book burnings were not merely attacks on ideas, but harbingers of violence against human beings. His astute observation reflected a profound understanding of a historical pattern: when regimes attempt to silence knowledge, they often escalate to silencing its bearers.

On May 10, 1933, Hitler's regime organized mass book burnings across the country, with the most infamous event taking place at Berlin's Opernplatz. However, similar burnings occurred in cities such as Munich, Frankfurt, Hamburg, Dresden, Leipzig, and Göttingen, among others. These acts, led by Nazi student groups and supported by propaganda minister Joseph Goebbels, targeted works by Jewish, socialist, and "un-German" authors such as Albert Einstein, Sigmund Freud, and Erich Maria Remarque — including Heine himself.

The book burnings marked the beginning of a darker chapter, foreshadowing the regime's transition from ideological purges to the unfathomable atrocities of the Holocaust, where the metaphorical burning of ideas became the literal burning of people.

15. Emily. J. M. Knox (2015). *Book Banning in 21st-Century America*. Rowman & Littlefield Publishers, London.
16. https://pen.org/book-bans/pen-america-index-of-school-book-bans-2023-2024/
17. Eli Pariser (2011). *The Filter Bubble. What the Internet Is Hiding From You.* The Penguin Press, New York.
18. Jonathan Haidt (2024). *The Anxious Generation: How The Great Rewiring of Childhood Is Causing An Epidemic of Mental Illness.* Penguin Books, London.

Chapter 7

When Mood Becomes Reality: The Danger of Emotional Truth

I can't listen to that much Wagner. I start getting the urge to conquer Poland.

— Woody Allen

In the early hours, the village lay in a serene slumber, cradled by the gentle whispers of the jungle night. The villagers, barefoot and half-asleep, turn their heads to the sky as the faint rumble of an approaching storm echoes in the distance. It is not the wind, it is not the rain — no, this is a man-made storm, a mechanical god with spinning blades and steel teeth, rising over the horizon with the first light of dawn. Then comes the music.

A distant sound echoes through the air, carried by the wind above the peaceful landscape of water buffalo and rice fields. It begins as a faint violin whisper, barely audible. Then the horns burst forth. Above, UH-1 Huey helicopters fill the sky, their silhouettes brightening against the morning sun. Inside the lead helicopter, Lieutenant Colonel Kilgore stands confidently in the open doorway, shirtless beneath his flak vest. His cavalry hat casts a shadow, partially obscuring the grin on his face. He breathes deeply, savoring the mingled scents of salt and napalm in the humid air.

"Raise it up," he commands, and the brass of "Ride of the Valkyries" echoes its war cry through the loudspeakers. The soldiers in the helicopters straighten their backs, grip their rifles tighter, their boots tapping involuntarily to the rhythm. The music makes them feel untouchable, invincible — gods descending onto the battlefield. Below, the village erupts into chaos. Mothers grab their children, farmers run from their fields, while monks clutch their prayer beads. Kilgore raises his hand.

"Now" – *mis*siles detached from the gunships, slicing through the air in a deadly arc. The first huts burst into flame, thatched roofs exploding into the sky in a shower of embers. Machine guns spit fire from the open doors of the helicopters, and the music soars higher, drowning out the screams. The palm trees bend under the force of the explosions. While the Valkyries ride through the sky, their song mingles with the crackle of burning wood and the distant cries of the wounded. Watching the destruction below, Kilgore smiles and states: *"I love the smell of napalm in the morning!"*

The famous helicopter attack scene from Francis Ford Coppola's *Apocalypse Now* (1979) is a cinematic masterpiece, in which Richard Wagner's music transforms the absurdity of war into an aesthetic experience. Originally part of Wagner's epic cycle of songs in *Die Walküre,* the music depicts the Valkyries, mythical warrior maidens of Norse legend, who ride across the battlefield to collect the souls of fallen heroes.

Picture 8. Helicopters from *Apocalypse Now*

By incorporating Wagner's music, Coppola elevates the helicopter attack into a kind of operatic ballet, with helicopters moving in formation, resembling dancers in a deadly performance. The music glorifies the action and imbues it with an emotion that is larger than life. To the viewer, the ensuing devastation seems more mythical than brutal. War is glorious and beautiful, as Wagner's music seduces us to believe. How ingenious Coppola's interpretation is; the Valkyria has accompanied various conflicts dating back from World War II from the nickname of B-17 Bombers to Germans assault *Operation Mercury* on Crete in 1941. In 1944 it was used as a codename to the failed assassin attempt of Adolf Hitler and disarming the SS groups by Colonel Claus von Stauffenberg.

After the war and due to the influence of Coppola's film, Wagner's music finally become a symbol of American military supremacy. Following the cinematic setting of *Apocalypse Now*, Black Hawk helicopters blared the "Ride of the Valkyries" during the American invasion of Grenada in 1983; in 1991, a psy-ops unit played Wagner during *Operation Desert Storm*, especially in the *Battle of 73 Easting*, instilling determination to the battle tank crews; and in 2004, while American Humvees rolled through the streets of Fallujah, "Ride of the Valkyries" once again echoed the strength and determination of the American military.[19]

Prior to this development, the historical foundations of Wagnerism as a symbol of war and power were, however, firmly established during the 1930s by the Nazi regime. Although it would be unjust to hold the composer Richard Wagner responsible for this association — he had already died 47 years earlier — the connection between his daughter-in-law, Winifred Wagner, and Adolf Hitler undeniably accentuated the perceived mythical violence in Wagner's music. In her role as the director of the Bayreuth Festival, Winifred Wagner actively endorsed the prevailing ideologies of the era. Notably, she is reputed to have provided paper and other supplies to Hitler during his imprisonment in Landsberg prison in 1923, when he penned his infamous book, *Mein Kampf*. The Bayreuth Festival of the 1930s, along with Wagner's music, subsequently evolved into an annual celebration of Nazi ideology. While there is an undeniable historical association between Richard Wagner's work and the National Socialist Party of the 1930s, it is crucial to recognize that Wagner's significance is far greater than this sad and cruel period in German history.

Richard Wagner (1813–1883) was not just a composer; he was a visionary whose influence on twenty-first-century Western culture remains profound. A cornerstone of Richard Wagner's legacy is the revolutionary concept of *Gesamtkunstwerk*, or "total artwork." This groundbreaking idea strives to seamlessly blend various art forms, such as music, drama, literature, visual arts, and architecture into a single, cohesive expression. Through this integration, Wagner sought to craft a holistic artistic experience that transcends the mere sum of its individual components. His approach was meticulously designed to establish a deeper psychological and emotional connection with the audience, immersing them in a multi-sensory journey intended to evoke a profound state of catharsis. By skillfully interweaving these artistic elements, Wagner aspired to create an overwhelming and transformative experience capable of leaving an indelible mark on the audience's psyche.

In order to create this experience in practice, Wagner uses the *leitmotif,* a recurring musical theme that symbolically represents characters, emotions, or ideas within his operas. Unlike simple repetition, Wagner's *leitmotifs* are dynamic, evolving in harmony, rhythm, and orchestration to reflect the unfolding drama. This evolution allows the motifs to interact and transform throughout the narrative, crafting a rich tapestry of sound that adds multiple layers of psychological depth to the storytelling. Wagner's art changes the psychological state of listener's emotions associated with mood. When a mood is sustained over time (Wagner's operas last usually 3.5 to 5 hours and his Ring Cycle 16 hours) it can reshape reality itself.

Mood is the silent architect of belief, whether through music, art, propaganda, or shared social experiences, it can altogether create the emotional foundation on which entire worldviews are built. For Wagner, that worldview was a utopia of new *Deutschtum* as a combination of true genuine *purest* art and *strong men* with high morals. This goal would be achieved through rituals symbolizing national unity and great artistic genius. If you control people's emotions, you don't need to justify your words, as you have already won the battle for their souls. This was the essence of Wagnerism, which fascinated and inspired Hitler most in his quest for world domination.

In 1933, after Hitler came to power, these Wagnerian elements were introduced in the Nuremberg rallies. The gatherings, orchestrated by the Nazi regime, utilized Wagnerian *leitmotifs* to evoke a sense of overwhelming anticipation, strength and unity. The gigantic scale of the festivals in its turn reflected the idea of the *Gesamtkunstwerk*, in which military prowess, civil morale-boosting, and breathtaking theatrical performances were put together reflecting the core values and ethos of *Deutschtum*. The mastermind architect of the events, Albert Speer, designed the structures in Zeppelin field — the grounds of the festival — to follow the ancient Pergamon altar, underlining the ritualistic and pagan elements of the festival. As evening turned to night, Speer's creative genius brought to life *Lichtdom*, the Cathedral of Light.

Picture 9. The Cathedral of Light

The rallies' aesthetic and psychological impact was so profound that they swept attendees into a fervor of passion and unwavering support. As so many contemporary eyewitness accounts show, the psychology of mass gatherings affected even people who had nothing to do with Nazi ideology. One of these was a young Jewish historian who, despite her understandable apprehension towards Hitler, accompanied a friend to the 1933 Nuremberg Rally. During the visit she observed an endless procession of idealistic youths, uniformed soldiers, adoring women, and devoted elderly — all brilliantly costumed, meticulously rehearsed, and flawlessly choreographed.

As festive rituals preceded the highlight of the evening — the anticipation and excitement of Hitler's arrival — she found herself swept up in the momentum of the evening. She was carried along to a dramatic crescendo as the Führer descended from the skies in a small plane to land on the Zeppelin field and joined the crowd in shouting and saluting "Heil Hitler" with fervent enthusiasm. Years later, she was still appalled at her own behavior, unable to comprehend what compelled her to join in that extraordinary spectacle and the mood of the crowds.[20]

For Adolf Hitler, Richard Wagner's music was not just a preference, but a profound spiritual and ideological myth that seamlessly outlined his grandiose self-portrait and his views for Germany. In the last few days, as his administration crumbled around him, Hitler is said to have listened to Wagner's *Götterdämmerung*, especially "Siegfried's Funeral March," shortly before his own suicide. However, this was not the first time the March was played — following the catastrophic German defeat of Stalingrad in February 1943, the German Radio sent Wagner's *Götterdämmerung* (Twilight of the Gods) as a symbolic gesture of the news. The opera's conclusion describes the destruction of the gods and the collapse of their world — the central metaphor of the sixth army fall and the central turning point of the war.

As the defeat in Stalingrad dealt a serious impact on Nazi Germany, it dismantled their invincible illusion and proclaimed the beginning of prolonged retreat. By choosing Wagner's music, especially the apocalyptic conclusion of the Ring Cycle, the Nazi administration tried to develop the loss into mythical, tragic terms rather than to admit to military failure. This suggested that the defeat was not just a setback, but a part of a broader historical drama — a story about the Führer, who was chosen to lead the other gods to the end of the world.

What is for sure is that most of the victims of World War II (an estimated 70 to 85 million people) had never heard of Richard Wagner and his music. A simple person might ask, what happened? The answer: The war broke out due to the long, prolonged negative social mood driven by fear, leading to rise of authoritarianism and then rationalized by pseudohistorical philosophy.

The overall mood in society is not a reaction to events — on the contrary, social mood shapes how events unfold before they even happen. These emotional tides rise and fall in waves, repeating over time but always in slightly different ways. While social mood cannot be forced, it still can be recognized and used by those who understand its power. Some take advantage of the moment, amplifying emotions to serve their own goals. In the hands of those seeking control, social sentiment can become a powerful weapon.

Authoritarian leaders thrive in times of uncertainty and fear. They adjust their message to match the prevailing negative mood, presenting themselves as the only source of stability. When people feel lost or disillusioned, these figures offer certainty, security, and the promise of a return to greatness. Their strength lies in turning collective emotions into a necessity, making obedience feel like the only path to survival.

However, social mood is not only a tool for control — it can also drive transformation. When optimism grows and people believe change is possible, movements emerge that challenge authority rather than strengthen it. The same energy that fuels authoritarian rule can also ignite resistance and revolution. The key question thus is not just who controls the mood of the moment, but what purpose it serves. Understanding power above all means understanding mood, not as a simple reflection of history, but as a battleground where the future is shaped. As already mentioned, the social mood chooses the leaders of the era. Our task should be to be aware of this.

19. Alex Ross (2020). *Wagnerism. Art and Politics in the Shadow of Music*, pp. 603–608.
20. Davis, M., Dulicai, D., and Viczian, I. (1992). "Hitler's movement signature," *The Drama Review 36*: p. 152.

Chapter 8

Once Upon a Time...

Picture 10. Neuschwentein and Disney Castles

Dream, believe, dare, do.

— **Walt Disney**

In fernem Land, unnahbar euren Schritten,
liegt eine Burg, die Montsalvat genannt;
ein lichter Tempel stehet dort inmitten,
so kostbar, als auf Erden nichts bekannt;

Drin ein Gefäß von wundertät'gem Segen
wird dort als höchstes Heiligtum bewacht:
Es ward, daß sein der Menschen reinste pflegen,
herab von einer Engelschar gebracht;

Alljährlich vom Himmel eine Taube,
um neu zu stärken seine Wunderkraft:
Es heißt der Gral, und selig reinster Glaube
erteilt durch ihn sich seiner Ritterschaft.

Wer nun dem Gral zu dienen ist erkoren,
den rüstet er mit überird' scher Macht;
an dem ist jedes Bösen Trug verloren,
wenn ihn er sieht, weicht dem des Todes Nacht.

Selbst wer von ihm in ferne Land' entsendet,
zum Streiter für der Tugend Recht ernannt,
dem wird nicht seine heil'ge Kraft entwendet,
bleibt als sein Ritter dort er unerkannt.

So hehrer Art doch ist des Grales Segen,
enthüllt - muß er des Laien Auge fliehn;
des Ritters drum sollt Zweifel ihr nicht hegen,
erkennt ihr ihn - dann muß er von euch ziehn.

Nun hört, wie ich verbotner Frage lohne!
Vom Gral ward ich zu euch daher gesandt:
Mein Vater Parzival trägt seine Krone,
sein Ritter ich - bin Lohengrin genannt.

Far and away, unapproachable to your steps
There is a castle called Montsalvat;
In the middle there stands a luminous temple,
As precious as nothing else on earth is known.

A vessel of miraculous blessing
Is guarded inside as supreme sanctuary.
It has been brought down by a host of angels,
To be cared for by the purest human beings.

Annually a dove from above approaches
To reinforce its miraculous power;
Its name is Sangrail, and it grants blissfully purest believe to its knighthood.

Who is predestined to serve the Sangrail
It prepares with supernal power;
Every evil's deception is lost to him,
When he sees it, death's power vanishes;

Even to him who is sent by it to alien lands,
Appointed as fighter for virtue's justice,
His holy power will not be taken away
If he goes unrecognized there as its knight.

May the Sangrail's blessing be ever of so noble cast,
It must flee the layman's eyes when it is unveiled.
Therefore you shall not doubt the knight,
If you recognize him - he has to leave you.

Now listen, how I reward the forbidden question:
By the Sangrail I was sent to you:
My futher Parzival wears its crown,
His knight, I - am called Lohengrin.

Standing at the top of the Bavarian mountains, a castle rises as if conjured from a dream: Neuschwanstein, the embodiment of medieval legend and longing. With its soaring towers and enchanting silhouette, it draws inspiration from the mythic tales that once captivated King Ludwig II, the so-called "Fairy tale" or "Swan king." From his childhood, Ludwig was enthralled by the legend of Lohengrin, the swan knight — a figure deeply intertwined with his lineage. The swan, both the heraldic symbol of Schwangau and the mystical emblem of Lohengrin, became an integral part of his identity. Yet his fascination deepened in 1861, when he first witnessed Wagner's Lohengrin at the Munich Court Opera House. The knight's divine mission, his aura of secrecy, and his tragic departure struck a chord with Ludwig's romantic ideals.

Determined to bring his vision to life, Ludwig began construction of Neuschwanstein Castle on September 5, 1869. The foundation stone was laid in 1872, and by the following year, the gateway building was completed, allowing Ludwig to stay on-site as he oversaw its progress.[21] But like Gaudí's Sagrada Família in Barcelona, his dream remained unfinished at the time of his death in 1886.

A century after, another traveler arrived in the Bavarian mountains. This mysterious visitor, though seemingly an average American tourist, carried with him a visionary's dream. Some say he came in 1935, others in 1955, but his presence, much like Lohengrin's, was cloaked in mystery. As he stood before Neuschwanstein, he must have felt its quiet magic, its fairy-tale towers rising beyond time itself. Perhaps he saw not just a castle, but a place ripe for a new beginning. When he left, he carried its magic with him, creating a new legend that would keep dreams alive for those who believe in magic. This visitor was no one else than Walt Disney.

Walt Disney's vision for Disneyland seemed to emerge like a dream, stitched together from fragments of memory, adventure, and longing. Perhaps it began on that park bench in Griffith Park, Los Angeles, where he watched his daughters ride the carousel, sensing the mood of a typical amusement park. Or perhaps it took shape as he wandered through Tivoli Gardens in Copenhagen, Denmark, admiring the seamless combination of fantasy and sophistication. Echoes of Neuschwanstein Castle, mingled with his fascination for nostalgia and European arts and music, inspiring him to create a place where the past and the future could coexist. Disneyland is not merely an amusement park — it is a portal to the collective imagination, a realm where stories come to life. *When you believe in a thing, believe in it all the way, implicitly and unquestionably,* Disney is said to have declared, embodying the very spirit of his work.

The essence of mood is paramount to the creative process; in fact, it may well be its cornerstone. Creativity transcends mere skill or intellect, while it is driven by an emotional undercurrent — by passionate belief, electrifying excitement, or a deep longing that sparks the energy to bring new ideas to life. If mood can shape legends, inspire monumental creative endeavors, and even steer the course of history, it's clear that mood is not just essential to creation — it is the invisible force that propels ideas into reality. Beyond its role in the creative process, social mood also influences the types of cultural products that thrive at specific moments in time.

Disney's productions tend to flourish during periods of positive social mood, when optimism, risk-taking, and escapism are dominant forces in society. During times of economic prosperity and cultural upswings, Disney's animated fairy tales and uplifting, family-friendly stories thrive. For instance, during the Great Depression and subsequent recovery of the 1930s, *Snow White and the Seven Dwarfs* (1937) emerged as a beacon of escapism, offering hope during a time of widespread hardship. Similarly, in the 1950s, the post-World War II boom gave rise to *Cinderella* and *Sleeping Beauty,* as well as the launch of Disneyland, all of which reflected a wave of social optimism that characterized the era.

This pattern continued throughout the 1980s and 1990s, during a period of economic expansion and the dot-com boom, when Disney's Renaissance films — *The Little Mermaid, Beauty and the Beast,* and *The Lion King* — captured the imagination of audiences, reinvigorating the company and reflecting the upbeat cultural mood of the time. In the 2010s, following the recovery from the financial crisis, films like *Frozen, Moana,* and the resurgence of *Avengers* and *Star Wars* franchises signaled a return to heroic storytelling, marking another era of optimistic and escapist narratives.

Socionomics, the study of how social mood influences collective behavior, suggests that entertainment trends mirror the prevailing sentiment of the masses. While positive social mood fosters light-hearted and optimistic storytelling, negative mood leads to darker, fear-driven narratives. This cyclical relationship is clear in the film industries. Mirroring the success of Disney productions, horror movies tend to surge in popularity during periods of negative social mood, when economic downturns, political instability, and heightened social anxiety create an atmosphere of uncertainty and fear. These films serve as a cultural reflection of prevailing anxieties, offering audiences a way to process and externalize their collective fears.[22]

The 1970s were a turbulent time, characterized by economic stagnation, political turbulence, and societal change. Amidst these challenges, psychological horror films like *The Exorcist, The Texas Chainsaw Massacre,* and *Halloween* rose to prominence. These movies effectively captured the prevailing sense of fear about societal collapse and the loss of control, introducing themes of invisible or unstoppable malevolence that resonated powerfully with audiences of the time.

Similarly, the 2000s mirrored this pattern in the wake of the post-9/11 atmosphere of fear and the economic downturn. This period saw the emergence of found-footage and torture-horror genres, with films like *Saw* and *Paranormal Activity*. These films reflected the increasing anxieties about surveillance, brutality, and human suffering. By tapping into the cultural zeitgeist, these horror films explored the vulnerabilities and fears of their respective eras, revealing a society grappling with uncertainty and existential dread. As fear and uncertainty gripped society, another genre also gained prominence: the rise of fictional heroes who stood as beacons of hope in dark times. Just as horror films mirrored public anxieties, superhero narratives provided an antidote — stories of justice, resilience and redemption.

In the late twentieth and early twenty-first centuries, characters like Batman emerged as symbolic saviors, confronting crime, corruption, and chaos in a world that often felt ungovernable. Films such as *The Dark Knight* (2008) captured this tension, portraying a society teetering on the edge of collapse while a lone hero fought to restore order. In times of heightened fear, the popularity of these heroic figures reflects a deep cultural yearning for stability, protection, and the belief that, even in the darkest moments, salvation remains possible. In the 2020s, shaped by the COVID-19 pandemic, social division, and economic uncertainty, there has been a resurgence of dystopian and existential horror. Films like *Nope, Smile,* and *Hereditary* delve into themes of societal collapse, paranoia, and the fear of an uncontrollable world. In these darker phases of social mood, horror cinema serves as a mirror to public anxieties, channeling collective fears into narratives of helplessness, isolation, and the unknown. A standout example of this is Todd Phillips's *Joker* that became a global box-office sensation in 2019, grossing over a billion dollars and surpassing Warner projections. Though marketed as a superhero origin story centered on Batman's iconic adversary, the film notably lacked any superheroes and refrained from the high-octane, CGI-driven (computer-generated imagery) action sequences typical of the genre.[23]

Controversial from the outset, the film prompted some theaters to ban audiences from wearing clown masks or costumes, a precaution born from fears that its violent and rebellious undertones might incite real-world disturbances. This caution mirrored the response to *A Clockwork Orange* (1971), where the film's graphic violence and iconic characters' look led to public backlash and some theaters choosing to withdraw the film. In both cases, the provocative nature of the content sparked fears about its influence on viewers, resulting in restrictions aimed at preventing misinterpretation or copycat behavior.

Reflecting on my experience of watching *Joker* in November 2019, I was truly captivated by the film's dark and foreboding mood. As the credits rolled and the film concluded, an unusual silence enveloped the audience, leaving no trace of smiles or casual chatter. This profound stillness seemed almost surreal, highlighting the film's powerful impact. Although I couldn't fully grasp the entirety of its message, it was evident that the movie delved deeply into themes of despair. The last scene of the film in particular bothered me. What kind of social mood would such a dark film reflect?

> After murdering a talk show host on live television, Arthur (the main character of the movie) is arrested and taken away in a police car as Gotham City erupts into riots. Protesters in similar clown masks flood the streets, looting and setting fires. As Arthur sits in the back of the squad car, he gazes out the window, seemingly mesmerized by the anarchy unfolding around him.
>
> Suddenly, an ambulance crashes into the police car, freeing Arthur. The rioters pull him from the wreckage and place him on the hood of the vehicle, cheering for him as their symbolic leader. As blood drips from his mouth, Arthur slowly rises, smears the blood into a twisted grin across his face, and dances triumphantly, basking in the chaos he has created.

When the Capitol incident, commonly referred to as the January 6 attack on the US Capitol, occurred, I immediately experienced a memory backlash to the final scene of *Joker*. Perhaps it was due to my socionomical imagination, but the words of Oscar Wilde echoed in my mind: "Life imitates art far more than art imitates life."

This idea, expressed in his 1889 essay *The Decay of Lying*, suggests that our perceptions and experiences are shaped by artistic representation rather than the other way around. Wilde argued that art provides the lens through which people interpret and understand reality. Mood, indeed, matters. Fortunately, in addition to the negative, there is also a positive direction, as we will see in the next chapter.

21. https://www.neuschwanstein.de/englisch/palace/history.htm?utm_source=chatgpt.com
22. Prechter, Robert (2012). "Film genres and social mood" in *Socionomic Studies of Society and Culture*. Socionomics Institute Press, pp. 127–139.
23. Booker, M. K. (2023). *No Joke: Todd Phillips's Joker and American Culture*. Liverpool University Press.

Chapter 9

Navigating the Tides of History

Time and tide wait for no man.

– **Geoffrey Chaucer**

In 1988, during a period when Estonia was still under the strict control of the Soviet regime, extraordinary events unfolded that would reawaken the national spirit and, a bit later, contribute to the independence of three nations. Thousands of brave Estonians gathered in Freedom Square, uniting their voices in a harmonious chorus that defiantly resisted oppression. They sang the forbidden anthem, "Mu isamaa, mu õnn ja rõõm" (my fatherland, my happiness and joy), a tribute to patriotism and national identity together.

Just 76 kilometers (47.2 miles) to the north, this same melody resonated freely as the Finnish national anthem, composed by Fredrik Pacius in 1847. The hymn served as a poignant reminder of Estonia's own past, when the song was also the national anthem of an independent Estonia from 1920 until 1940, before the Soviet occupation. The forthcoming singing revolution, as it was later to be called, emerged and gained momentum, while it reached its crescendo at the Laulupidu, the Estonian Song Festival, in 1988.

The festival's roots stretch back to the Estonian national awakening, with the inaugural national song festival held in Tartu in 1869. Four years later it found a new home in Tallinn, and since 1928, it has become a cherished tradition every five years in July at the Lauluväljak (Song Festival Grounds) in the district of Kadriorg. With a rich history, this monumental event has showcased the harmonious voices of vast collective choirs, often featuring over 30,000 singers on stage, captivating audiences as large as 80,000 attendees.

Picture 11. Tallinna lauluväljak

Just as in Estonia, Finland's path to sovereignty around seventy years earlier had been also heavily influenced by its cultural and musical heritage. In the late nineteenth century, Finland was experiencing significant pressure from Russian rulers, especially after the February Manifesto was declared by Tsar Nicholas II in 1899. This decree greatly reduced Finland's historical autonomy, initiating what is known as the first wave of Russification.

The Russian Empire aimed to tighten its grip on Finland by enforcing Russian laws and language, challenging Finnish national identity and self-governance. In this politically charged environment, artists, journalists, and citizens stood in opposition to the Tsarist regime's policies. It was an unprecedented situation for an autonomous Finland, with its own governmental institutions, to witness the censorship of the press and the transformation of street names to reflect Russian influence.

Amidst a climate of cultural and political resistance, Jean Sibelius composed *Finlandia*, a symphonic poem that emerged as a potent symbol of defiance and national pride. This composition was crafted as a covert protest against Russian censorship and oppression, with its message so overt that it was initially banned. To circumvent this censorship and suppression by Russian authorities, the piece was later disguised under the innocuous title of "Impromptu."

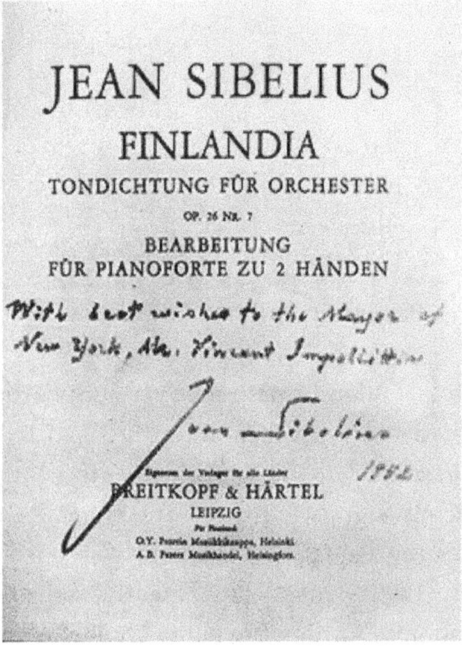

Picture 12. Finlandia, piano arrangement by the composer, 1952 autographed copy for the Mayor of New York.

Despite numerous attempts to suppress it, *Finlandia* emerged as a potent and unifying anthem for the Finnish national movement. It invigorated the spirit of resistance against the Russian Empire, not only elevating Sibelius' status as a revered composer but also drawing international attention to Finland's quest for recognition and independence among the world's nations. Through its stirring melodies and evocative themes, Sibelius' composition fostered a profound sense of solidarity and hope, playing a pivotal role in Finland's journey towards sovereignty. Much like it inspired Finland to achieve independence from Russia in 1917, *Finlandia* also played a significant role in helping Finland preserve its independence against the Soviet Union, while the lyrics to what was originally instrumental music were penned by the poet V. A. Koskenniemi. He crafted the poignant words for the hymn in 1940, amidst the onset of the Winter War. These lyrics capture the resilience and the mood of wartime Finland:

Oh Finland, behold, thy daylight is dawning,
the threat of night has now been driven away.
The skylark sings across the light of morning,
like the firmament itself was chiming,
and now the day the powers of night is scorning:
thy daylight dawns, oh fatherland!

Oh Finland arise, and raise towards the highest
thy head crowned with mighty memories
Oh Finland arise, for the world thou cries
That thou hast thrown off thy slavery,
Beneath oppression's yoke thou never liest.
Thy morning's come o motherland.

Since its premiere, *Finlandia* has maintained its reputation as one of Sibelius' most admired compositions. The piece's universal message, encapsulated in Sibelius' evocative tones, has led to its adaptation with various lyrics for diverse settings. In the United States, it is performed in the American Presbyterian Church, and members of the Mormon faith often play it on the organ within their tabernacles. The hymn has even served as the National Hymn of Biafra, a short-lived African state from 1967 to 1970 in the eastern region of Nigeria. Notably, American conductor Leopold Stokowski once suggested that it should be adopted as the world's national anthem. However, only few might know that it also played a pivotal role in igniting the Singing Revolution in the Baltics, where, once again, it fulfilled its historic mission as a beacon of freedom.

In the summer of 1988, three distinct festivals — *Tartu Pop Festival, Eesti Vabaks* rock festival, and the time-honored *Laulupidu* — converged to tell a shared story of defiance, hope, and unity. It might be challenging, perhaps even unnecessary, to pinpoint which of these festivals was most radical. However, what is unmistakable is the transformation in the nation's collective mood. No longer were the people gripped by fear, indifference, cynicism, or submission, with a bleak outlook on the future. Instead, they embraced fearlessness, active involvement, optimism, and a profound hope for the possibilities of tomorrow.

In Tartu, the old national flag was displayed publicly for the first time. The *Eesti Vabaks* Rock Summer Festival, popularly known as "Glasnost Rock – Rock for Peace," in its turn, defied the strict policies of the communist authorities regarding what kind of songs could be played, while rock musicians spontaneously performed the music they wanted to play. The Finnish rock band Leningrad Cowboys, visiting the festival, with their unique hairstyle and anarchist humor, openly mocked communism.

At the climax of the concert, the singer of the Leningrad Cowboys, Sakari Kuosmanen, dressed as a sumo wrestler, decided to take a risk and sang the *Finlandia* anthem alone. This time, ending it with the words: *Thy morning come* ESTONIA![24] As the crowd went wild, Sakari wondered what the militia would do. Despite the police witnessing his actions, their uncertainty in handling the situation probably spared him from imprisonment.

Last but not least there was the Laulupidu, a festival that was not part of the regular five-year cycle in 1988 and thus not a state-sanctioned event that year. However, it was a spontaneously improvised popular assembly, cleverly disguised as a concert. Over 300,000 people gathered to sing together, and between the songs, key political figures gave speeches advocating sovereignty and national self-determination. In all of the events, soviet soldiers and police stood by, silently watching

Picture 13. Leningrad Cowboys

the dramatic change in people's mood from the sidelines. There was a new determination and sense of unity in the air that transcended individual concerns and painted a vivid picture of a society ready to embrace change and chart its own course.

Although extraordinary events occurred at various festivals that foreshadowed a significant change in history, no Soviet troops could stop this, no government could silence an entire nation singing in unison. A few years later, Estonia would stand on its own. But in the summer of 1988, Estonia was not yet free. It fought – through rock, folk, choral music, and eventually across three different countries. On August 23, 1989, a historic show of unity and determination was witnessed when some 2 million people joined together to form a human chain, stretching 675 kilometers (420 miles) across the Baltics, from Tallinn, Estonia, through Riga, Latvia, to Vilnius, Lithuania. And they were singing.

This event, known as the "Baltic Way," commemorated the 50th anniversary of the Molotov-Ribbentrop Pact, which led to the Soviet occupation of the Baltic states. In 1990 to 1991, when all three Baltic states had declared their independence, the Soviet Union had to relent and recognized their independence on September 6, 1991. The prevailing sense of freedom and self-determination ultimately won out, leading to a transformation of the entire geopolitical landscape of Eastern Europe. As the Baltic states sang their way to freedom, mood conquered matter.

As a postscript, on June 12, 1993, Helsinki's Senatorial District became the stage for a once-in-a-lifetime event, when the eccentric Leningrad Cowboys and the distinguished Red Army Choir, featuring an impressive assembly of 180 singers and musicians, performed for 70,000 people. The audience witnessed the seemingly impossible when the Soviet Army Choir sang *Finlandia* in Finnish.

The audience felt the historical weight in every note of the anthem, as the choir, dressed in the Soviet military uniform, showed respect and friendship for their western neighbor. In dramatic contrast, the Leningrad Cowboys took the stage in their turn and burst into "Let's work together," a classic rock anthem. The transition from *Finlandia* to the energetic rock beat was outrageous, unexpected, and full of joy. The audience roared with appreciation and sensed that something truly unique had just happened.

After the Helsinki concert, the entire Balalaika show toured Tallinn, Riga, Minsk and finally Moscow, including a performance in Red Square. No wonder, for a moment, the confrontation between East and West seemed to have disappeared like a bad dream.

However, the transformative wave of change was not orchestrated by the likes of Sibelius, the Leningrad Cowboys, Mikhail Gorbachev, or any single influential figure. Rather, every person, as both a participant and an observer, was swept by the rising tide of a powerful social mood that reshaped their future.

Picture 14. Total Balalaika Show

First, social mood emerges. Then it carries people along with it in accordance with the currents of history… And so, as we observe the currents of social mood, the ebbs and flows of collective sentiment, it becomes clear that history is not merely a series of events to be witnessed, but a mirror reflecting the possibilities within ourselves. Each cycle, each wave, carries with it lessons of caution, but also glimpses of opportunity. In recognizing these patterns, we are offered not just understanding but also a quiet empowerment: the chance to act with awareness rather than drift in unconscious repetition.

24. https://youtu.be/A7PN1ZJDhqo?feature=shared

Chapter 10

Social Mood, Fear and Media

Men are not afraid of things, but of how they view them.

– Epictetus

The Boston Daily Globe

RADIO PLAY TERRIFIES NATION

The Capital Parade

Lehman Expects Poletti Victory

READY FOR HALLOWEEN

3 FIRES SET IN SO. END HOTEL

PATROL WAGON, AUTO CRASH

Mars Invasion Thought Real

Hysteria Grips Folk Listening In Late

Many Fear World Coming to End

Police, Youth Groups Plan Safer and Saner Halloween

FAIL TO CLAIM

POLICE, BRIDAL

Mystery Veils Fatal Injuries

Picture 15. Radio play terrifies nation

On October 30, 1938, CBS Radio's *The Mercury Theatre on the Air* captured the attention of its audience by broadcasting H. G. Wells' science fiction story *The War of the Worlds*. This radio program was ingeniously disguised as a series of news bulletins that created the illusion of a real-time, unfolding catastrophe. Originally presented as a standard music program, the broadcast was occasionally interrupted by dramatic reports of an alien invasion. Delivered so authentically, many listeners who tuned in missed the crucial disclaimer that the program was entirely fictional.

As radio reports vividly described Martians landing in New Jersey, widespread panic spread among the unsuspecting public. As the broadcast progressed, eager listeners across the country reacted to the "news" with shock and disbelief. Some fled their homes, seeking refuge in basements or nearby towns, while others flooded local police stations with calls, desperate for information and guidance.

In New York, where the broadcast wielded a particularly potent influence, a woman dramatically interrupted a church service, hysterically proclaiming the end of the world. Many others huddled by their radios, gripped by sheer terror, with some even resorting to wearing gas masks or arming themselves, utterly convinced that an attack was imminent. The pervasive mood of fear, amplified by the tense geopolitical climate, made Orson Welles' fictional broadcast of a Martian invasion strikingly believable. This landmark event catapulted Welles into the national spotlight, setting the stage for his illustrious career in Hollywood. His newfound fame enabled him to craft cinematic masterpieces such as *Citizen Kane, The Magnificent Ambersons,* and *Touch of Evil,* making him one of the most iconic directors in the film industry.

The War of the Worlds, as well as Welles' other psychological insights, inspired a pioneering researcher of media science, Marshall McLuhan, in his seminal work *Understanding Media: The Extensions of Man.*[25] According to McLuhan's well-known phrase, *the medium is the message,* the intrinsic characteristics of a medium shape human experience more profoundly than the content it conveys. For instance, the advent of the printing press not only catalyzed literacy and individualism but also transformed societal structures by enabling the mass dissemination of information.

A bit later, TV and worldwide live satellite broadcasts ushered in a new era of interconnectedness and an awareness of global simultaneity. This transformation is vividly captured in his concept of the *global village,* where electronic media dissolve geographical boundaries, fashioning a world where real-time connectivity mirrors the instantaneous communication within the human nervous system. According to McLuhan, media acts as an extension of the human senses, fundamentally altering perception, cognition, and social structures of the public audiences. In this context, media not only facilitates communication but also redefines cognitive frameworks and interpersonal dynamics. And thus, it also amplifies the social mood.

In this respect, our own Internet era is much stronger than its predecessors. Following McLuhan's ideas, technology and social media play a significant role in the collective emotionality of our time. The message of this media is sensationalism, outrage, and immediacy of emotional reactions, which outweigh thoughtful consideration and reflection, regardless of the topic. At the same time, pervasive connectivity and the sheer volume of information we encounter daily are contributing to fragmentation and a profound lack of critical analysis in public debate.

The dawn of the *Homo sentients* era is evident in many aspects of life, as the era of *Homo sapiens* fades away – especially in decision-making, opinions, and the pursuit of truth. While in the past, political and social debates were (or at least expected to be) based on reasoned arguments and empirical evidence, today, intuition, emotion, and personal narrative play a more central role in discussion. Public policy and governance are now shaped more by public sentiment than by data-based assessments of what might be objectively true or wise. Another development is the increasing subjectivity of truth.

While the Enlightenment emphasized objectivity, scientific reasoning, and the pursuit of knowledge without personal prejudice, in contemporary society truth is increasingly determined by individual perceptions and group consensus. The rise of relativism, in which multiple conflicting "truths" coexist, challenges the notion of universal principles and undermines intellectual debate, while authority is increasingly derived from identity rather than from reasoned expertise. In the past, argumentation and debate were based on logic and facts, but today the legitimacy of views is often judged on the basis of personal experience and emotional appeal.

As we navigate this new era, the challenge lies in ensuring that emotional engagement doesn't come at the cost of reason and facts. With the collective social mood now at its highest peak, hubris and arrogance have emerged as socially acceptable behaviors. However, this arrogance is likely to be followed by an inevitable decline. Being arrogant means that you don't actually trust yourself and the future, and that arrogance is a way to cover up your insecurities. At first, the gradual erosion of social sentiment may go unnoticed, but when fear finally takes hold of society, extreme things will follow that no one can ignore or even avoid. Social mood divides and drives the reality, not rationality.

Let's talk about COVID-19 and compare it to the Hong Kong Flu of 1968–1969. Did you notice a lightning-fast mood change in yourself when COVID was mentioned? Disclaimer, we can do just a simple calculation on the differences between Hong Kong Flu and COVID-19, step by step.

Step 1: Calculate death rates (%):
To compare the significance of deaths in relation to world population, we first calculate the percentage of deaths for both pandemics.

Hong Kong Flu[26] *(1968–1969)*:

- Estimated deaths: 1–4 million
- World population (1968): 3.55 billion
- Death rate (%) = (Deaths / Population) × 100
    - Low estimate: (1,000,000 / 3,550,000,000) × 100 = 0.028%
    - High estimate: (4,000,000 / 3,550,000,000) × 100 = 0.113%

COVID-19[27] (2019–2023):

- Confirmed deaths: 7 million (WHO), but excess deaths could be 15–20 million
- World population (2019): 7.7 billion
    - Low estimate: (7,000,000 / 7,700,000,000) × 100 = 0.091%
    - High estimate: (20,000,000 / 7,700,000,000) × 100 = 0.26%

Step 2: Set up Pearson's t-test:
To statistically compare the death rates of the two pandemics, we perform an independent two-sample t-test. The null hypothesis (H_0) assumes no significant difference in death rates, while the alternative hypothesis (H_1) assumes a significant difference.

We use the estimated death percentages as our datasets. I'll now run the Pearson t-test.

Step 3: Pearson's t-test results:

- t-statistic: -1.11 (negative sign indicates the difference in means, but we focus on magnitude)
- p-value: 0.416

Step 4: Interpretation of the test:

- The p-value (0.416) is greater than 0.05, meaning we do not have enough statistical evidence to conclude a significant difference between the death rates of the Hong Kong Flu and COVID-19.
- While COVID-19 had a higher absolute death toll, its death rate relative to world population does not significantly differ from that of the Hong Kong Flu at a 95% confidence level.

Discussion

As pandemics have consistently shaped human history, the governmental responses have reflected the political, technological, and societal contexts of their time. Even though the 1968 Hong Kong Flu and the COVID-19 pandemic both resulted in casualties globally, the responses to these crises were vastly different. The reaction to the Hong Kong Flu was notably weaker than that of COVID-19 due to differences in medical advancements, public perception, global interconnectedness, and governmental intervention.

In 1968, influenza pandemics were perceived as inevitable and largely uncontrollable. Despite vaccine availability, mass immunization was not prioritized, and drastic interventions like lockdowns were not considered necessary. Public perception, influenced by a slower media environment, did not drive urgent demands for action. Furthermore, international travel was not restricted, and any quarantine measures were not implemented. In contrast, the response to COVID-19 included travel restrictions, lockdowns, and mass vaccination campaigns, supported by an infrastructure capable of handling large-scale public health measures. The public discussions were censored and the working conditions of entrepreneurs, artists and musicians etc. were effectively blocked.

Table 3. **Key differences from COVID-19 response**

Factor	COVID-19 (2019–2023)	Hong Kong Flu (1968–1969)
Lockdowns	Widespread global lockdowns	No major lockdowns
Vaccine timeline	2020 (1 year)	1969 (1 year)[28]
Public restrictions	Strict, all-encompassing	Few, mild
Travel bans	Many international bans	No major bans
Government role	Large-scale intervention	Limited intervention

Why was the response weaker in 1968?

1. In 1968, the overall social mood was positive.
2. Different public attitudes: Flu was expected and not seen as a global emergency.
3. Lower media influence: No Internet or 24/7 news cycle to spread fear.
4. Less globalization: Travel was more limited, so disease spread slower.
5. Milder economic disruptions: No major supply chain shocks like in COVID-19.

How much money was used to prevent the disease?
While the 1968 costs are estimated to be $50 billion in today's terms,[29] the COVID-19 pandemic has likely cost between $10 trillion to $16 trillion in total worldwide.[30] In summary, 320 times more funds were used to combat COVID-19 than for Hong Kong Flu. As COVID-19 restrictions were lifted progressively, with WHO and governments leading the decisions, influenced by scientific data, economic pressures and public demand; today, COVID-19 is treated as an endemic disease, similar to the flu, rather than an emergency.

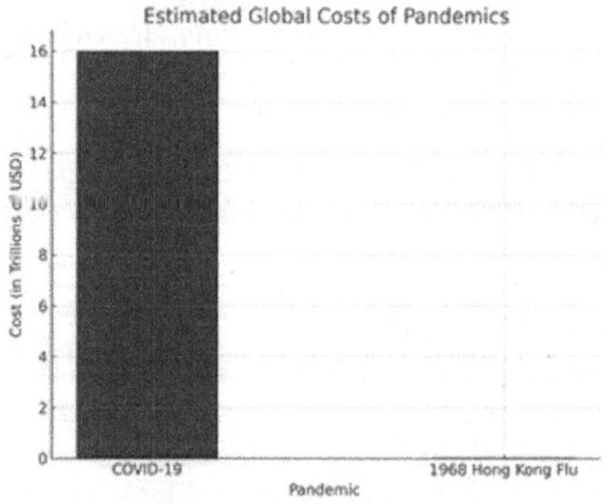

Chart 2. Estimated global costs of pandemics

The unanswered question is whether those measures were really necessary and what else could the $16 trillion have been used for? Well, for example:

Medical and disease eradication:

- Malaria[31]: $16 trillion could fund 16,000 years of malaria control programs.
- Tuberculosis[32] (TB): Ending TB worldwide would cost around $13 billion per year, meaning we could have eradicated TB for centuries.
- HIV/AIDS: The global budget for HIV/AIDS programs is about $20 billion per year.
- Universal vaccination programs: Every child in the world could have received vaccines for common diseases many times over.

Scientific and technological advances:

- Cancer research: Global cancer research funding is about $200 billion per year – $16 trillion could have advanced treatments dramatically.
- Antibiotic resistance research: One of the biggest looming threats, yet funding is limited.
- AI and biotech for disease prediction and prevention: Cutting-edge technologies could revolutionize public health.

Infrastructure and global well-being:

- Clean water and sanitation for all[33]: To meet the water, sanitation, and hygiene (WASH) targets of Sustainable Development Goal 6 by 2030, an annual global investment of approximately $114 billion is needed.

- Global food security: $330 billion could end world hunger for 10 years.[34]

I am speechless for a moment. Although the amounts mentioned in different sources vary and are, of course, educated guesses … nothing in the details really change the fact. I wonder, is this an *irrational exuberance* or … sheer madness of the crowds? In the light of rational analysis, the single biggest reason for the chosen policy was herd behavior based on the negative social mood that was reinforced by social media.

Let's be careful the next time someone starts to talk to us about Mars, shall we?

25. Heyer, Paul. (2003). "America Under Attack 1: The War of the Worlds, Orson Welles, and 'media sense'," *Canadian Journal of Communication 28*: pp. 149–165.
26. https://www.britannica.com/event/1968-flu-pandemic?utm_source=chatgpt.com
27. https://www.worldometers.info/coronavirus/?utm_source=chatgpt.com
28. Jester, B. J., Uyeki, T. M., and Jernigan, D. B. (2020). "Fifty Years of Influenza A(H3N2) Following the Pandemic of 1968," *American Journal of Public Health, 110*: pp. 669–676.
29. Jinjarak, Y., Noy, I., and Ta, Q. (2022). "Pandemics and Economic Growth: Evidence from the 1968 H3N2 Influenza," *Economics of Disasters and Climate Change, 6*: pp. 73–93. https://doi.org/10.1007/s41885-021-00096-1
30. Cutler, D. M., and Summers, L. H. (2020). "The COVID-19 Pandemic and the $16 Trillion Virus," *JAMA, 324*: pp. 1495–1496. https://doi.org/10.1001/jama.2020.19759
31. https://www.theglobalfund.org/en/
32. https://www.theglobalfund.org/en/tuberculosis/?utm_source=chatgpt.com

33. https://www.worldbank.org/en/topic/water/publication/the-costs-of-meeting-the-2030-sustainable-development-goal-targets-on-drinking-water-sanitation-and-hygiene?utm_source=chatgpt.com
34. https://www.iisd.org/articles/iisd-news/ending-world-hunger-2030-would-cost-330bn-study-finds?utm_source=chatgpt.com

Chapter 11

The Myth of Educational Superpower

Every great advance in science has issued from a new audacity of imagination.

— **John Dewey**

About a decade ago, I had the opportunity to visit Teachers College at Columbia University in New York, where I was invited to deliver a lecture and exchange ideas with American colleagues. Founded in 1887, Teachers College is situated in the historic neighborhood of Morningside Heights at West 120th Street, within Columbia University's distinguished campus. As I stepped through the entrance of the college, the institution's rich history and academic prestige were immediately apparent. Despite the welcoming atmosphere, security was notably stringent. I underwent a screening and was issued a guest pass with my photo, granting me access to navigate the building and proceed to the lecture room.

On the entrance hall wall, my attention was drawn to a quote from John Dewey's *My Pedagogical Creed*: "Education is the fundamental method of social progress and reform." This statement resonated with the college's mission, underscoring the vital role of education in society. Dewey's philosophy emphasized the importance of social consciousness in forming individual perceptions, advocating for an educational system that fosters collective responsibility and societal reform.

The following morning, I was taken aback to find out that my access pass had expired, necessitating yet another round of comprehensive security checks, complete with a fresh photograph and passport verification. When I inquired about the security protocols, my hosts explained that these measures were put in place to address the rising incidence of school shootings in the United States. They also subtly suggested that the profitability of the security industry might influence the state of the affairs. Yet, the very next day, when I visited the Faculty of Humanities to meet a Finnish colleague in a building just across the street, I was taken aback by the absence of any security measures. This contrast led me to ponder whether different academic disciplines, especially humanities, are viewed with varying degrees of value and significance?

Teachers College at Columbia University has long stood as a beacon of educational leadership in America, spearheading pivotal movements and addressing critical issues. As someone with a keen interest in music and arts education, I found its rich history truly captivating. According to prominent Dean of Harvard and Professor of American Educational History, Ellen Lagemann, to understand American education in the twentieth century, one must recognize that the ideas of Edward L. Thorndike prevailed over those of John Dewey.[35] Both were teachers at Teachers College, and their different views continue to influence education even today.

John Dewey (1859–1952) and Edward Thorndike (1874–1949) represented opposing educational philosophies that continue to influence American schooling. Dewey championed experiential, student-centered learning, advocating for an education that fosters critical thinking, creativity, and social responsibility. He believed that learning should be rooted in real-world experiences, with students actively engaging in problem-solving rather than passively absorbing information. Progressivists like Dewey argued that traditional schooling stifles curiosity and fails to adequately prepare students for the complexities of modern life.

In contrast, Thorndike emphasized efficiency, standardization, and measurable outcomes, laying the foundation for the modern testing movement. His behaviorist principles influenced policies like the No Child Left Behind Act and Common Core standards, which prioritize rigorous content mastery and objective assessments. Traditionalists, following Thorndike's vision, argue that disciplined instruction and academic excellence are essential for accountability and long-term success. They contend that an overemphasis on creativity and open-ended learning risks undermining foundational knowledge, leaving students unprepared for higher education and the workforce.

This ideological divide manifests still in ongoing policy debates. Standardized testing, a hallmark of traditionalist education, is criticized for reducing learning to a series of metrics — yet these tests remain deeply embedded in education systems worldwide. Meanwhile, progressive approaches, despite their appeal, often face resistance due to concerns over assessment reliability and educational rigor. Schools and policymakers frequently struggle to strike a balance, attempting to integrate innovative pedagogies while maintaining accountability.

During my visit, Finland was hailed as a global leader in education, renowned for its seamless integration of both traditional and innovative educational frameworks. Finnish students consistently ranked highly in the PISA (Program for International Student Assessment) results, which led to a steady influx of educators from around the world eager to learn from Finland's education system. While countries like Singapore and Canada also performed exceptionally well, Finland stood out not just for its academic achievements but for its holistic approach to education. Prioritizing equity over competition, Finland fostered a system with minimal standardized testing, highly trained teachers, and a strong emphasis on student well-being and creativity. Unlike the rigid, exam-driven models of some high-ranking nations, Finland's success was built on trust in educators, later school start ages, and a balanced approach to learning — making it a widely admired, though often difficult-to-replicate model for the rest of the world.

However, beneath the surface of Finland's educational success, a quiet dispute was brewing – largely unnoticed by the broader public. While Pasi Sahlberg's *Finnish Lessons* series (2011, 2012, 2015) gained international acclaim, Gabriel Sahlgren's *Real Finnish Lessons: The True Story of an Education Superpower* (2013)[36] received much less attention. In his work, Sahlgren challenged the prevailing narrative, arguing that Finland's education system was neither as exceptional nor as universally applicable as widely believed. He pointed to factors such as a homogeneous population and distinct educational policies as key contributors to Finland's high performance.

I recall Sahlgren predicting that the shift from traditional, teacher-led instruction to pupil-centered, inquiry-based methods could undermine students' cognitive development and overall academic achievement. He stressed the importance of maintaining a hierarchical educational structure, where teachers retain authority and guide students through structured, knowledge-based learning. According to Sahlgren, Finland's initial success stemmed, at least in part, from its traditional teaching methods, making its future decline a likely consequence of moving away from them.

Pasi Sahlberg dismissed publicly Sahlgren's argument as nonsense (*ihan* höpöhöpöä[37] in Finnish), stating that he wouldn't have accepted Sahlgren's work at Harvard – nor even as a master's thesis at the University of Helsinki. I found this amusing. In the end, the Finnish education debate wasn't much different from the American one. While I didn't take a position on whether Sahlgren's thesis met academic standards or not, it was clear that his affiliation with the market-liberal Centre for Policy Studies likely irked Sahlberg. Universities have always been selective about who gets to address certain issues and how they are framed. The notion that ideas argue, not people, quickly falls apart – especially when scientific controversies are often as much about personal dynamics as they are about facts.

What comes to shifts in major social mood sentiments, education is not an exception. What are the best methods, what is the school culture like, should students be taught traditionally or led to self-direction? Opinions vary, but ultimately only time can be the most reliable judge of which predictions will prove correct. Let's face it, Finland is no longer the educational superpower it was a decade ago. Although Gabriel Sahlgren seems to win the debate, it doesn't mean that Pasi Sahlberg's ideas were wrong. The gap between educational theory and practice is wide, and they evolve over time. Since my own perspective was already shaped by socionomics, I could sense the signs of change in 2014 — after a peak of optimism and the inevitable hype, a downturn always follows.

The socionomic model of explaining the popularity of education is consistent with wave theory: in periods of optimism and growth, societies tend to favor progressive educational philosophies, such as student-centered learning, creativity, and innovation. These shifts align with societal desires for change, freedom, and individual expression, which are characteristic of an upward, positive mood phase. During such times, educational reform often emphasizes flexibility, inclusivity, and the idea that education should prepare students to think critically and adapt to a rapidly changing world.

Conversely, during pessimistic or crisis phases, the focus often shifts back to more traditional educational values. In these periods, there is a societal longing for stability, discipline, and a return to "core knowledge" or teacher-centered instruction. These phases typically reflect a desire to reassert control and structure in the face of uncertainty, mirroring the regressive turn in many aspects of culture and policy during negative social moods.

Since educational ideologies do not evolve linearly, but rather cycle in waves, they reflect larger cycles of social mood. These fluctuations may align with broader historical and economic cycles, such as the booms and busts seen in financial markets. This cyclical nature suggests that changes in educational beliefs are not just the result of rational, evidence-based decision-making, but are deeply influenced by the prevailing social mood and collective psychology of the time.

As long as we remain in the herd, these discussions will continue, while a real solution would require rare courage to think against the prevailing mood, and with the eyes of an impartial witness.

35. Lagemann, E. C. (1989). "The Plural Worlds of Educational Research," *History of Education Quarterly* 29: pp. 185 214.
36. https://cps.org.uk/wp-content/uploads/2021/07/150410115444-RealFinnishLessonsFULLDRAFTCOVER.pdf
37. https://www.hs.fi/maailma/art-2000002867292.html

Chapter 12

From Semper Augusta to "Everything Bubble"

I can calculate the motion of heavenly bodies, but not the madness of people.

— **Sir Isaac Newton**

Picture 16. Semper Aurora

In the seventeenth century, at the heart of the Netherlands, Amsterdam stood a vibrant hub of trade, wealth, and freedom. The city's harbors brimmed with ships bearing treasures from the East Indies, while its banks safeguarded immense fortunes. A beacon of optimism and liberalism, Amsterdam welcomed a wave of new ideas and exhibited a remarkable tolerance for thinkers from less liberal parts of Europe. Many famous philosophers such as Baruch Spinoza, René Descartes, and John Locke — among many others — found a haven within its borders. As wealth and prosperity flourished, a simple yet magnificent flower, the tulip, had been in the Netherlands since 1562, having originated in Turkey.

At the beginning it captivated mostly the noblemen and merchants with its vibrant crimson petals, but over time, the allure of the flower spread across social strata, causing the prices of tulip bulbs to soar. By 1634, tulip mania had swept through Dutch society with an almost feverish intensity, transforming these delicate blooms into symbols of wealth, power, and prestige. The affluent families of Amsterdam began to covet tulip bulbs, and their gardens were transformed into stunning showcases of extravagance.

Among these prized possessions was the illustrious *Semper Augusta*, celebrated for its striking white petals boldly streaked with vivid red and gold hues. Its rarity only added to its allure, propelling its value to unprecedented levels. Stories of the tulip craze quickly spread throughout the bustling city as rumors abounded of individuals trading entire estates for a single *Semper Augusta* bulb. In the lively taverns, merchants eagerly recounted tales of fortunes amassed from the tulip trade. They spoke of contracts, promises forged in the heat of the moment, and bulbs anticipated to double in value by the next season.

Caught up in the frenzied atmosphere, people conflated the act of purchasing flowers with securing their financial future. In the heart of the marketplace, the auctioneer's gavel continuously drove tulip bulb prices to dizzying heights. A *Semper Augusta* could command prices of 10,000 guilders, then soar to 20,000, earning its moniker as the "golden flower." Amidst this frenzy, few questioned the developing madness, for the promise of quick riches was too tempting. However, this mania did not affect everyone. Those who happened to return to Holland after a long absence did not necessarily notice it or understand what was going on. Sometimes this ignorance could lead to strange situations — as there are various versions of the following story, it is likely to be true.

A prosperous merchant, who was a devoted collector of rare tulips, had recently received a valuable shipment of goods from the Levant. A sailor, tasked with delivering the news of its arrival, approached the merchant at his counting house, bearing reports of bales filled with various merchandise. In gratitude for the sailor's message, the merchant generously offered him a red herring for breakfast. The sailor, having a fondness for onions, noticed what appeared to be an onion bulb on the counter, seemingly out of place amidst the silks and velvets. Mistaking its true nature, he pocketed it to accompany his herring.

Unbeknownst to him, the bulb was a precious *Semper Augusta* tulip, valued at 3000 florins, equivalent to about £280 sterling. Once the sailor had departed, the merchant discovered the absence of his prized bulb. Panic ensued throughout the establishment as frantic searches yielded no results. Eventually, someone recalled the sailor's presence. The distraught merchant dashed into the street, followed by his worried household.

The unsuspecting sailor, oblivious to the commotion, sat contentedly on a coil of ropes, savoring the last bite of his "onion." Little did he realize that his breakfast had cost more than enough to feed an entire ship's crew for a year.[38] However, while the sailor was imprisoned under investigation, the next morning, February 3, 1637, the Tulip Mania market crashed. Investors who had once eagerly bought up the rarest bulbs were now withdrawing, and their wealth was rapidly disappearing. On that day, the famous Semper Augustus bulb, which had been as valuable as a luxurious mansion, suddenly fell to a fraction of its value. The tulip craze ended, and many lost their entire fortunes as it vanished like smoke into thin air.

Despite this historic crash, tulips have remained one of the most beloved symbols of the Netherlands. Every spring, millions of tulips bloom in the country's fields, painting the landscape in shades of red, yellow and purple. The Keukenhof Gardens are a major attraction for flower enthusiasts, with 1.5 million visitors from around the world. Known as the "Garden of Europe," the park is home to over 7 million tulips each year, offering a unique and immersive experience of Dutch horticulture. Even if tulips do have economic importance for the Netherlands, perhaps their true value lies in the joy and color they bring to people's lives?

Picture 17. The splendor of Keukenhof. Photo provided by Keukenhof Gardens

Although the tulip mania is often cited as one of the earliest examples of a speculative bubble, it was neither the first nor the last in history. A "Boom-Bust Cycle" or a "Bubble Lifecycle," is a well-recognized pattern that speculative markets tend to follow. The cycle commences with the Stealth Phase, where early adopters and insiders quietly begin investing, sensing potential where others might not yet see it. As the cycle progresses into the Awareness Phase, a broader public begins to take notice, largely fueled by increasing media coverage that highlights the growing opportunity. Next, the Mania Phase unfolds, characterized by a frenzy of speculation as investors rush to buy into the asset, often driven by the belief that "this time is different" and that the asset's price will only continue to rise. This surge of enthusiasm reaches a crescendo during the Euphoria/Peak stage, where the asset becomes vastly overvalued, and savvy investors, known as smart money, begin to exit their positions, capitalizing on the inflated prices.

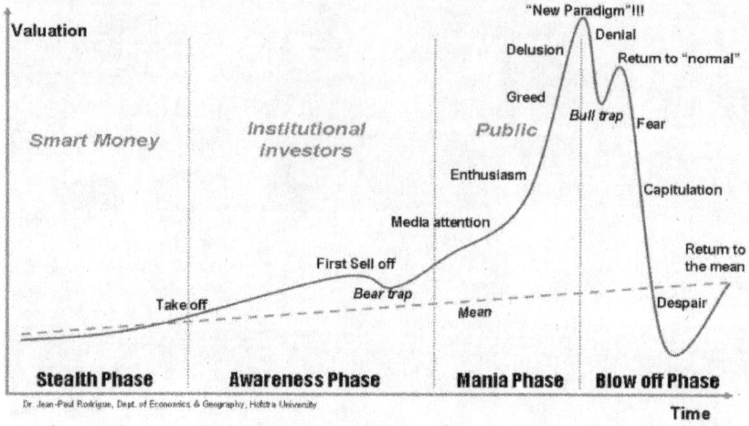

Picture 18. Boom/ bust cycle

However, the cycle invariably turns as reality sets in, leading to the Blow-off Phase. Here, panic selling ensues as investors scramble to offload their assets, realizing that the prices were unsustainable. This panic is followed by the Despair/Trough stage, where prices crash below their intrinsic value, creating a temporary floor before stabilization occurs. Finally, the cycle concludes with a rebound, where the market begins to recover, driven by the reassertion of fundamental values that support a more sustainable price level. This recovery sets the stage for potential future growth, completing the cycle and providing lessons for the next wave of speculative activity.

This sequence has happened often throughout history, despite those who believe in their investments and assure themselves "this time it's different." The most significant financial asset bubbles and crashes can be found in the following list:

- The Dutch tulip bulb bubble (1636)
- The South Sea bubble (1720)
- The Mississippi bubble (1720)
- British canal mania (1790s)
- Latin American and bond bubble (1820s)

- The British railway mania (1840s)
- The Panic of 1857 (global financial crisis)
- The Panic of 1873 (long depression)
- The Australian land boom and bust (1880s–1890s)
- The Panic of 1893 (railroad and banking collapse)
- The Panic of 1907 (US banking crisis)
- The Russian Revolution and hyperinflation (1917–1922)
- The late 1920s stock price bubble (1927–1929)
- The Great Depression (1929)
- The surge in bank loans to Mexico and other developing countries (1970s)
- The silver market bubble (1979–1980, Hunt brothers' attempt to corner the market)
- The bubble in real estate and stocks in Japan and in Nordic countries (1985–1989)
- The Black Monday stock market crash (October 19, 1987)
- The bubble in real estate and stocks in Thailand, Malaysia, Indonesia, and several other Asian countries (1992–1997)
- The surge in foreign investment in Mexico (1990–1993)
- The dot-com bubble (1995–2000)
- The Russian financial crisis (1998)
- The Argentine economic crisis (1999–2002)
- The US housing bubble (2002–2007)
- The global financial crisis (2008)
- The European sovereign debt crisis (2010–2012)
- The Chinese stock market crash (2015–2016)
- The Bitcoin and cryptocurrency boom and bust (2017–2018)
- The COVID-19 market crash and recovery (2020)
- The SPAC and tech stock bubble (2020–2021)
- The bond market turmoil (2022)
- The speculative boom in AI and tech stocks (2023–)

… And finally, the "Everything Bubble."

The "Everything Bubble" refers to the speculative excesses of our time, which owes its existence to the grand monetary experiment orchestrated by the Federal Reserve and other central banks. For more than a decade, ultra-low interest rates and successive rounds of quantitative easing have flooded financial markets with cheap money, inflating asset prices across stocks, bonds, and real estate alike. This era of boundless liquidity has fostered a peculiar illusion — an age of effortless prosperity in which wealth seems to materialize without toil or productive enterprise — "the greatest virtual wealth ever created."

The seeds of the Everything Bubble were sown in the aftermath of the 2008 financial crisis. To prevent economic collapse, the Federal Reserve under Ben Bernanke, later succeeded by Janet Yellen, adopted policies of ultra-low interest rates and quantitative easing (QE). The rationale was clear: cheap money would stimulate borrowing, investment, and economic growth. Yellen continued this approach, emphasizing the need for low rates and liquidity injections to sustain expansion.

The COVID-19 pandemic accelerated this dynamic. Jerome Powell, as Fed Chair, responded with unprecedented stimulus, pushing QE to new heights and slashing interest rates to near zero. Trillions in fiscal stimulus, combined with an expansionist monetary policy, led to asset price inflation across the board — the defining feature of the Everything Bubble. While Yellen believed in sustained economic intervention to ensure growth, Powell, once a champion of easy money, was forced to reverse his view when inflation started to surge after the COVID-19 crisis. Rising prices and supply chain disruptions revealed the dangerous side effects of prolonged monetary stimulus. By 2022, Powell signaled a major shift, launching an aggressive rate hike campaign to combat inflation. This rapid tightening of financial conditions exposed the fragility of the system. Stocks, which had reached record highs, tumbled. The housing market cooled. The collapse of Silicon Valley Bank and other regional lenders in 2023 highlighted the vulnerability of institutions dependent on low rates. The Everything Bubble, which has inflated over a decade, began to deflate.

While mainstream economists like Yellen and Powell have focused on controlling inflation, Robert Prechter has long argued that the real threat is deflation, not inflation. As a proponent of Elliott Wave theory, Prechter believes that economic cycles follow a predictable pattern, driven by social mood shifts. According to his theory, the Everything Bubble was a natural extension of a euphoric wave of optimism, and its bursting will bring a prolonged deflationary collapse.[39] Deflation, in Prechter's view, occurs when debt defaults and credit contractions overwhelm central bank interventions. When the Everything Bubble fully pops, it will lead to a self-reinforcing cycle of falling asset prices, bank failures, and economic contraction. Consumers and businesses, overleveraged and debt-ridden, will be forced to sell assets at distressed prices, triggering further declines. If Prechter is correct, Powell's rate hikes may have inadvertently set this cycle in motion. As the Everything Bubble deflates it can happen either two ways:

1. A controlled soft landing — Powell and policymakers attempt to stabilize the system with liquidity injections, rate cuts, and fiscal stimulus, hoping to prevent a deep recession.
2. A full-blown deflationary collapse — credit contracts, markets crash, and economic despair sets in, leading to a prolonged downturn similar to the Great Depression.

Given the cyclical nature of social mood, history suggests that economic downturns are associated with political and social upheavals. The 1930s brought fascism and war; the 1970s led to economic stagnation and political realignment. If the Everything Bubble mirrors these past cycles, we may now be on the verge of a new era of economic and political transformation. What that might be is anyone's guess, the crucial question is whether policymakers can prevent a deflationary spiral or whether we are destined to repeat the economic crashes of the past.

The phrase commonly attributed to Mark Twain, "History does not repeat itself, but it rhymes," means that even the events of history may not occur in exactly the same way – similar patterns, themes, and cycles tend to emerge over time. "Pride goeth before destruction, and a haughty spirit before a fall" (Book of Proverbs 16:18), warns that excessive arrogance or overconfidence often leads to downfall. It suggests that when individuals, nations, or institutions become too self-assured and disregard caution, they set themselves up for failure.

According to socionomics this is called hubris, which can usually be perceived by an outsider only...

38. Maccay, Charles. (1852). *Memoirs of Extraordinary Popular Delusions and the Madness of Crowds*, p. 92.
39. Prechter, Robert R. (2002). *Conquer the Crash, You Can Survive and Prosper in a Deflationary Depression.* New York: John Wiley & Sons.

Concluding Remarks

This book centers on waves of social mood and their profound influence on cultural, political, and economic transformations. While social phenomena may seem unpredictable and chaotic at first glance, they are, however, deeply connected to the collective psyche of society, reflecting its shifting moods. Despite the historical context and external variations, social phenomena follow patterns, making them not only observable but also, to some extent, predictable.

While much of academic literature begins with predefined theory, then gathers information, and ends with real-life examples to validate the theoretical model, this book takes the opposite approach. Here, human experience in real-life context comes first — whether this experience is felt through rock music, moments of hope and despair, the emotional pulse of daily life, the joy of a revolutionary singing, or the anxieties amplified by media. Afterward, these experiences are examined through the lens of social mood theory and explained by a coherent rationalization. Since all cultural interpretations are subjective, it is up to the reader to assess the validity of the conclusions.

The concept of *Homo sentiens* — which views humans as inherently emotional beings driven by their feelings and perceptions — offers, in my view, a deeper understanding than traditional rational analyses of individual behavior. People do not act based on pure logic; very often they act on how they feel and particularly when they are a members of a group, they amplify their shared mood through herding impulse. Thus, in a world where social sentiment drowns out reason and public opinion shifts like the wind, understanding the tides of collective emotion is more crucial than ever. The collective events are dependent on the collective mood of the society.

Because social mood is a collective phenomenon rather than an individual trait, it is more enduring than shorter experienced personal emotions. While individual emotions can be influenced, social mood — being preconscious and cyclical — cannot. Instead, it shapes our perception of reality itself. Woven into every moment of individual and collective life, social mood shapes beliefs, customs, and habits. Once felt, it is later rationalized into ideas, art, monuments, literature, and other cultural expressions. To truly understand our world, we must first grasp the emotional landscape of culture — since in every great idea, monument, or movement lies a feeling that set it all in motion. However, since there is no single "right" way to see the world or interpret works of art, the ability to understand and engage with different — even opposing — perspectives is a mark of wisdom and a cornerstone of democracy.

Although the essays selected for this book are grounded in generally known historical facts and influenced by Robert Prechter's pioneering work in socionomics, my interpretations are mainly shaped by my personal experiences (among the many books I have read). For those interested in exploring socionomic theory in its orthodox form, I recommend my book *Socionomics: How Social Mood Shapes Society,* a concise 140-page scholarly presentation of Prechter's central ideas. However, a word of warning: those who have read it have found it complicated, but those who have read it three times have found it truly insightful.

As we bring this exploration to a close, I would like to share some additional reflections on *Waves of Change: A Study of Social Mood*. I'll revisit key ideas from each chapter, offering fresh insights and suggesting further reading for those interested in delving deeper. I hope this section will encourage you to continue exploring social mood, sparking your curiosity about how it shapes not only our world but your own experiences as well.

It All Starts with Pop Music

The first chapter is based on my personal observations from Finland. In the summer of 2006, when I first became acquainted with Prechter's thinking, the prevailing mood in my country was highly optimistic. This optimism was reflected in external signs such as Finland's Eurovision victory by Lordi, success in ice hockey at the Olympics, and the peak of Nokia's stock price. After reading Prechter's *Conquer the Crash* book, I anticipated the downturn to come soon. As that downturn unfolded two years later through the financial crisis of 2008, my research plan on pop music began to take shape. The research presented in this chapter has been published in both the *Popular Music*, Cambridge, and as a chapter in the book *Mood*, part of the Warwick series in humanities by Routledge.

If you're interested in exploring pop music and its relationship to social mood more, as well as the future of the music business, I recommend a quite recent book by Liz Pelly, *Mood Machine: The Rise of Spotify and the Cost of the Perfect Playlist*. It's not difficult to imagine that changes in social mood can already be measured through Spotify traffic. While the role of live music continues to decline side by side with the negative "anti" social mood, the mood that normally would be shared in public places, now spreads through digital environments. However, if social mood were to rise again and live concerts and in-person gatherings increased, a more positive social mood would be shared again in a live situation.

Mapping Growth and Decline

Fibonacci numbers play a crucial role in Elliott Wave analysis. The Fibonacci sequence (0, 1, 1, 2, 3, 5, 8, 13, 21, etc.) is closely tied to market behavior, as it reflects natural patterns that appear in financial movements. Elliott identified that the proportions of wave movements often align with Fibonacci ratios, such as 61.8%, 38.2%, and 1.618. For instance, Wave 2 in an impulse pattern often retraces 61.8% of Wave 1, and Wave 3 is frequently

1.618 times the length of Wave 1. These ratios help analysts predict key price levels and retracements in a market cycle.

Fibonacci numbers are also used to predict the timing and extent of market movements. Fibonacci time ratios (e.g., 1, 2, 3, 5, 8, 13, 21) are applied to forecast how long specific waves will take. In addition to retracements, Fibonacci extensions (such as 161.8%, 261.8%) help predict the potential length of waves, particularly in the case of Wave 3, which often extends beyond Wave 1. These tools allow traders to anticipate price levels and time frames for both trend continuation and reversals, enhancing their ability to navigate market cycles effectively.

In addition to the modern applications of Fibonacci numbers in market analysis, the origins of these mathematical principles are deeply rooted in history, notably through the works of Luca Pacioli and Leonardo da Vinci. Pacioli, a fifteenth-century Italian mathematician and Franciscan friar, is often regarded as the "father of accounting" for his work on double-entry bookkeeping. However, he also played a pivotal role in introducing Fibonacci's sequence to the Renaissance world in his famous work, *Summa de Arithmetica*. This book, which Pacioli co-authored with da Vinci's illustrations, highlighted the practical applications of mathematics in various fields, including art and engineering.

Leonardo da Vinci, known for his genius in both art and science, was influenced by Pacioli's teachings on mathematics, particularly in his works like the *Vitruvian Man,* which incorporates the Golden Ratio — a mathematical relationship closely tied to Fibonacci numbers. Da Vinci's use of this ratio in his art further exemplifies how deeply interconnected mathematics and human perception are, a concept that underpins much of what we explore today in social mood and market behaviors.

While there isn't a comprehensive biography solely focused on Elliott's life, his theories and writings have been compiled and discussed in several notable works:

Picture 19. Vitruvian Man

The Major Works of R. N. Elliott by Robert Prechter

- This compilation includes Elliott's key writings, providing insight into his development of the Wave Principle. It offers readers a direct view of his analytical methods and market observations.

Elliott Wave Principle: Key to Market Behavior by A. J. Frost and Robert Prechter

- This is the foundational text on the Elliott Wave theory, detailing the principles of wave patterns and how they reflect market psychology. Prechter, a key figure in the development of socionomics, provides a thorough explanation of Elliott's work.

The Psychology of Human Misjudgment by Charlie Munger

- While not directly related to Elliott Wave or Fibonacci, Munger's exploration of human psychology in decision-making can offer valuable insights into the behavioral patterns that drive social mood and market sentiment.

The Winds and Waves of War

This chapter is related to the history of my family on my grandparents' sides. Before World War II, they lived in the Karelian region, which after the Winter War of 1939–1940 and later the Continuation War of 1941–1944 had to be ceded to the Soviet Union. Although each country has its own historical peculiarities, the fate of today's Ukrainians reminds Finns of their own history. Apart from Great Britain, Finland was one of the few European countries that was not occupied during World War II.

A Frozen Hell: The Russo-Finnish Winter War of 1939–1940 by William R. Trotter

- The book offers a detailed narrative of the Winter War, focusing on the human side of the battle. It also explores the role of terrain and weather in the conflict, which were crucial factors in the outcome of the war.

The Winter Warriors (*Les Guerriers de l'Hiver*) by Olivier Norek

- Historical novel based on true events, which follows a small division of soldiers, farmers, and workers armed with outdated rifles, battling Stalin's Red Army. Led by an ex-legionnaire nicknamed The Horror and a young man destined to change history, they fight through the brutal winter. Amidst the carnage, a new legend is born — Simo Häyhä, known as The White Death.

The Essence and Phases of Mood

Although there are numerous manifestations of social mood, its basic distribution, explained in a nutshell, is as follows. Social mood arises naturally through human interaction. People are then induced to express it, identifying referents and inventing rationales to justify their mood-driven feelings and actions. These referents and rationales spread by contagion.

Socionomics views this process as a mutual interaction, not a one-way contagion, emphasizing that social attitudes develop through collective mimicking, with diverse outcomes based on social mood. Because socionomic theory is very broad, it may take some time to master. In addition to my own book, *Socionomics: How Social Mood Shapes Society,* I recommend two works that shed light on the subject from different perspectives:

The Wave Principle of Human Social Behavior and the New Science of Socionomics by Robert Prechter

- The book is a foundational text for understanding how social mood cycles influence human behavior and social trends. Prechter presents a detailed analysis of social mood phases and their impact on culture, politics, and economics.

The Tipping Point: How Little Things Can Make a Big Difference by Malcolm Gladwell

- This book explores how social moods shift and how small events or behaviors can trigger widespread societal changes. It's useful for understanding how collective emotions and moods evolve and influence society at large.

At the Highgate Cemetery

As a frequent visitor to London, I've come to know many of its suburban sights over the years. Highgate Cemetery, with its impressive Victorian architecture, is a must-see for history enthusiasts. I'll admit that when I visited two years ago, I was unaware of Litvinenko's grave.

I've selected these books because they are directly relevant to the chapter's topic:

Necropolis: London and Its Dead by Catharine Arnold

- The book explores the history of London's cemeteries, with significant focus on Highgate, discussing its origins, famous residents, and the cultural impact of Victorian burial practices.

A Very Expensive Poison by Luke Harding

- This is a detailed investigation into the assassination of Alexander Litvinenko. Harding, a journalist for *The Guardian*, provides an in-depth look at the poisoning, the Russian state's possible involvement, and the wider political implications of the murder. It's a well-researched, gripping account of a high-profile and controversial case that has had lasting effects on UK-Russian relations.

Freedom Versus Control

In general, there are four major types of censorship: withholding information, destroying information, altering or using selective information and self-censorship. Withholding information is a common form of censorship used by many governments throughout history. Beyond these four major types, censorship manifests in various forms:

1. Political censorship – Suppressing information that challenges the government or ruling authority, such as banning opposition media in authoritarian states.
2. Religious censorship – Restricting content that contradicts or criticizes religious beliefs, such as banning books deemed blasphemous.

3. Corporate censorship – Companies restricting speech to protect their interests, such as social media platforms removing controversial content.
4. Military censorship – Controlling information related to national security and warfare, such as blacking out sensitive war coverage.
5. Moral censorship – Restricting material deemed obscene or inappropriate, such as age restrictions on media.
6. Economic censorship – Controlling speech through financial pressure, such as advertisers pulling funding from critical news outlets.
7. Internet and digital censorship – Blocking or filtering online content, such as governments restricting access to certain websites.
8. Academic censorship – Suppressing ideas in education and research, such as restricting discussions on politically sensitive topics.
9. Cultural censorship – Controlling content to maintain social norms or values, such as editing foreign films to fit local standards.

Suggestive reading on this issue:

The Age of Surveillance Capitalism by Shoshana Zuboff

- Examines how corporate censorship and data control shape public discourse.

Fahrenheit 451 by Ray Bradbury

- A classic novel that explores the consequences of book burning and thought control.

When Mood Becomes Reality: The Danger of Emotional Truth

My personal connection to Richard Wagner's music began in 1991, inspired by a performance of *Parsifal* in Tampere Hall. Wagner's works were rarely performed in Finland in the post-war period, probably due to foreign policy self-censorship. Since the Soviet Union collapsed that same year, his operas came back into the repertoire in Finland. Inspired by the performance of *Parsifal*, the Finnish Wagner Society was founded the very same year.

Wagner Societies are international organizations dedicated to promoting Richard Wagner's music and legacy. Many societies offer priority access to Bayreuth Festival tickets, which are notoriously difficult to obtain due to high demand and a long waiting list. By joining a Wagner Society, it is one of the best ways to secure tickets to the festival through raffles for its members (I have been lucky twice).

If you are not yet familiar with Wagner, I highly recommend you watch the Stephen Fry documentary *Wagner and Me* produced by the BBC. As Fry has a Jewish background, he explores and struggles with the paradox of Wagnerian antisemitism, but ultimately sees Wagner's wonderful music as universal, arguing that its beauty should not be rejected due to its creator's flaws. Other suggestions are:

Albert Speer: Conversations With Hitler's Architect by Joachim Fest

- A collection of interviews with Albert Speer, Hitler's chief architect. The book delves into Speer's attempts to justify his actions, offering a psychological portrait of a man entangled in a fascist dictatorship while grappling with guilt and responsibility.

Wagnerism. Art and Politics in the Shadow of Music by Alex Ross

- Ross examines the profound influence of composer Richard Wagner on art, culture, and politics and his ideas that shaped both the nineteenth and twentieth centuries, impacting figures in literature, visual arts, and political movements.

Once Upon a Time...

I have never been to Disneyland – perhaps one day I will, if we are lucky enough to have grandchildren. However, as a Wagner enthusiast, I have traveled to all the Bavarian castles of Ludwig II. Like most essays in this book, each of these castles and themes could inspire entire books of their own. When it comes to cinema, its socionomic analysis plays a central role, alongside political and financial analyses of societies. Some tips for further reading:

Ludwig II of Bavaria: The Swan King by Christopher McIntosh

- A well-researched biography exploring Ludwig II's life, his obsession with fantasy and art, and his legacy.

Disney's Land: Walt Disney and the Invention of the Amusement Park That Changed the World by Richard Snow

- Focuses specifically on Disneyland and Disney's vision for themed entertainment.

Socionomic Studies of Society and Culture by Robert Prechter

- As a core book on the theme, *socionomic studies* offer a groundbreaking perspective on how collective social mood drives trends in culture, politics, and markets.

No Joke: Todd Phillips's Joker and American Culture by Keith Booker

- Booker offers a critical analysis within the broader context of American society. The book examines how the film reflects contemporary anxieties, political tensions, and cultural shifts, making it a valuable resource for understanding current social mood in the US.

Navigating the Tides of History

In 1987, when I first visited Estonia, there was only one ship sailing between Helsinki and Tallinn. The name of the ship was *Georg Ots*, after a famous Estonian singer. The same ship had served as accommodation a year earlier at the Reykjavik summit, where Ronald Reagan and Mikhail Gorbachev met to discuss nuclear disarmament.

Today, three different companies operate cruises between Helsinki and Tallinn, with a total of more than ten ships serving the route for approximately 7.5 million passengers annually. While in the mid-1980s there was a growing sense of cautious optimism in the country, the true socialist reality was still starkly visible in Tallinn. The Viru Hotel, where we stayed, was fitted with surveillance equipment, the shops were nearly devoid of goods, and the buildings were in a state of disrepair. For those who haven't experienced it, it's hard to fully grasp. History often fades, and today's Tallinn — with its towering skyscrapers and upscale stores — feels like a city from another planet.

The importance of the singing revolution in this historical transformation cannot be underestimated. In 1992, The Polar Music prize of one million Swedish kronor was uniquely awarded to the Baltic states of Estonia, Latvia, and Lithuania, recognizing their courage and resilience during their struggle for independence from the Soviet Union. This prestigious "Musician's Nobel" was established by Stig Anderson, the manager of ABBA, and it is awarded annually to individuals or groups who have made outstanding contributions to music, regardless of genre or field.

Previous Polar Music prize laureates include Paul McCartney, Bruce Springsteen, Peter Gabriel, Chuck Berry, Ennio Morricone, Led Zeppelin, Patti Smith, Stevie Wonder, Paul Simon, Kronos Quartet, Elton John, Metallica, Iggy Pop, Ravi Shankar, Renée Fleming, Miriam Makeba, Sofia Gubaidulina and Angélique Kidjo, as well as the conductor Esa-Pekka Salonen – the music director of San Francisco Symphony and conductor laureate of the Los Angeles Philharmonic, the Philharmonic Orchestra in London and the Swedish Radio Symphony Orchestra.

Recommended readings for this chapter are:

The Collapse of the Soviet Union by David R. Marples

- This book covers the events leading to the end of the Soviet Union, with a focus on the Baltic states and their role in challenging Soviet rule. It provides a broader, political context for the Singing Revolution.

Jean Sibelius and His World by Daniel M. Grimley

- A comprehensive exploration of Sibelius's music and its cultural, historical, and political context.

Social Mood, Fear and Media

Orson Welles and Marshall McLuhan were pioneers in understanding media's power to shape perception and influence emotions. Welles' *War of the Worlds* broadcast showed how mass media could induce fear, while McLuhan's insight that "the medium is the message" foresaw its deeper societal impact. Today, as media expands, a wealth of research confirms McLuhan's theories, showing how digital platforms, 24-hour news, and algorithms shape cognition and amplify emotions –

especially fear – just as they predicted. The books to read in relation to this chapter are:

Amusing Ourselves to Death: Public Discourse In the Age of Show Business by Neil Postman

- In this acclaimed classic, Postman examines how television, as the dominant form of media, transforms serious discussion into entertainment, leading to a society that values entertainment over critical thinking. The book examines how the media shapes perceptions of reality, often in the pursuit of sensationalism.

The Shallows: What the Internet Is Doing to Our Brains by Nicholas Carr

- "Is Google making us stupid?" Nicholas Carr asks in the book that focuses on the Internet's influence on cognition. According to the writer, the technologies we use to find, store, and share information can literally reroute our neural pathways. And thus, alter the way we process information and engage with media.

The Myth of Educational Superpower

During my trip to New York, I was awarded a scholarship to stay in a residence on 125th East Street, an apartment building frequented by jazz musicians and dancers. The location was convenient, situated near Columbia University and roughly the same elevation as Manhattan Island. After the evening lecture, my host and their group of doctoral students took me to a local pizzeria, and the evening unfolded smoothly.

At one point, someone asked the name of my hotel, and I mentioned the address of the residence. The room fell silent. Then, someone hesitantly asked, "Are you sure you meant the west side?" I had already noticed that I didn't encounter many white people like me in the area, but I hadn't quite grasped the implications. Perhaps I was naive, but I didn't know how to feel about it or even how to be afraid.

Other recommended reading:

Democracy and Education by John Dewey

- A cornerstone of progressive education, arguing for experiential, student-centered learning.

Experience and Education by John Dewey

- Dewey's later work, where he refines his views and responds to critiques of progressive education.

Left Back: A Century of Battles Over School Reform by Diane Ravitch

- A historical critique of progressive education and its impact on American schools.

From Semper Augusta to "Everything Bubble"

At the end of my university studies in 1991, the Finnish economy collapsed due to a banking crisis. Events progressed rapidly and several businesses and individuals went bankrupt. It is easy to admit that this experience has influenced my understanding of economic bubbles and the manias that precede them. As investment advisors often say, past performance is no guarantee of future performance. Having read Prechter's entire output, I put his book first on my list of recommendations:

Conquer the Crash, You Can Survive and Prosper in a Deflationary Depression by Robert Prechter

- In the book Prechter warns of an impending deflationary depression, advising readers on how to protect and potentially grow their wealth during such economic downturns. The book emphasizes the importance of safety and preparedness in the face of financial instability.

Manias, Panics, and Crashes: A History of Financial Crises by Charles P. Kindleberger and Robert Z. Aliber

- A comprehensive history of financial crises and speculative bubbles, illustrating how they follow predictable cycles of euphoria and collapse.

The Everything Bubble: the Endgame for Central Bank Policy by Graham Summers

- Argues that decades of central bank intervention have created an unsustainable global financial bubble, covering stocks, bonds, real estate, and more.

References

Bolton, H. (2018). *The Complete Elliott Wave Writings of A. Hamilton Bolton and Charles J. Collins:* with a foreword by Robert R. Prechter and a biography by A. J. Frost. New Classic Library, Gainesville, Georgia, USA.

Booker, M. K. (2023). *No Joke: Todd Phillips's Joker and American culture*. Liverpool University Press.

Breidenbach, B. and Docherty, T. (2019). *Mood. Interdisciplinary Perspectives, New Theories.* Routledge, New York and London.

Casti, J. (2010). *Mood Matters: From Rising Skirt Lengths to the Collapse of World Powers.* Copernicus Books, New York.

Cushman, F. (2020). "Rationalization is rational," *Behavioral and Brain Sciences 43*: pp. 1–59.

Davis, M., Dulicai, D., and Viczian, I. (1992). "Hitler's Movement Signature," *The Drama Review 36*: pp. 152–172.

Haidt, J. (2024). *The Anxious Generation. How the Great Rewiring of Childhood Is Causing An Epidemic of Mental Illness.* Penguin Books, London.

Harding, L. (2016). *A Very Expensive Poison.* Guardian Books, London.

Hayes M. H. S., and Patterson D. G. (1921). "Experimental Development of the Graphic Rating Method," *Psychological Bulletin 18*: pp. 98–99.

Heyer, P. (2003). "America Under Attack 1: The War of the Worlds, Orson Welles, and 'Media Sense'," *Canadian Journal of Communication 28*: pp. 149–165.

Jester, B. J., Uyeki, T. M., and Jernigan, D. B. (2020). "Fifty Years of Influenza A(H3N2) Following the Pandemic of 1968," *American Journal of Public Health, 110*: pp. 669–676.

Ketovuori, M. (2024). *Socionomics: How Social Mood Shapes Society*. Routledge, London.

Ketovuori, M. (2022). *Laumavaiston varassa.* Agile Publishing, Espoo.

Ketovuori, M., and Lampert, M. (2018). "From 'Hard Rock Hallelujah' to 'Ukonhauta' in Nokialand: a Socionomic Perspective on the Mood Shift In Finland's Popular Music from 2006 to 2009," *Popular Music, 37*: pp. 237–252.

Ketovuori, M. (2007). *Two Cultures of Arts Education, Finland and Canada? An integrated View.* Annales Universitatis Turkuensis, University of Turku.

Knox, E. J. M. (2015). *Book Banning in 21st-century America.* Rowman & Littlefield Publishers, London.

Lagemann, E. C. (1989). "The Plural Worlds of Educational Research," *History of Education Quarterly 29*: pp. 185–214.

Maccay, C. (1852). *Memoirs of Extraordinary Popular Delusions and the Madness of Crowds.* L. C. Page & Company [reprinted 1932].

McLuhan, M. (1964). *Understanding Media: The Extensions of Man.* McGraw Hill, New York.

Pariser, E. (2011). *The Filter Bubble. What the Internet Is Hiding from You.* The Penguin Press, New York.

Prechter, R. (2017). *Socionomic Studies of Society and Culture.* Socionomic Institute Press, Gainesville, Georgia.

Prechter, R. (2012). "Film Genres and Social Mood," in *Socionomic Studies of Society and Culture.* Socionomic Institute Press, pp. 127–139.

Prechter, R. (2016). *The Socionomic Theory of Finance.* Socionomic Institute Press, Gainesville, Georgia.

Prechter, R. (2002). *Conquer the Crash, You Can Survive and Prosper in a Deflationary Depression.* John Wiley & Sons, New York.

Prechter, R. (1999). *The Wave Principle of Human Social Behavior and the New Science of Socionomics.* New Classics Library, Gainesville, Georgia.

Ross, A. (2020). *Wagnerism. Art and Politics in the Shadow of Music.* 4th Estate, London.

Thorton, M. (2005). "Skyscrapers and Business Cycles," *Quarterly Journal of Austrian Economics 8*: pp. 51–74.

Van Baardwijk, M., and Franses, P. H. (2010). "The Hemline and the Economy: Is There Any Match?" *Report / Econometric Institute, Erasmus University Rotterdam*, pp. 1–11.

Zuboff, S. (2019). *The Age of Surveillance Capitalism. Profile Books, London.*

Endnote

Waves of Change: A Study of Social Mood is a collection of thought-provoking essays that explore the dynamic and powerful force of collective social mood. The ideas presented in it have their base in the author's previous publication *Socionomics: How Social Mood Shapes Society* (2024). *Waves of Change* offers an overview on how collective mood endogenously shapes everything, from political upheavals to cultural revolutions. With its wide-reaching implications, it is a must-read for anyone eager to understand how the prevailing mood of a time can drive events and change as well as redefining culture and societies. This book offers not just a key to understanding the course of history, but it also suggests how to anticipate the future.

About the Author

Mikko Ketovuori is a Finnish writer and former University Lecturer at the University of Turku, where he taught in the Department of Teacher Education. With a background that bridges education, cultural theory, and the social sciences, his work explores how collective mood shapes society, politics, and the arts. He is the author of *Laumavaiston varassa* (2022), a bold inquiry into herd instinct and the fragility of institutional life, and *Socionomics: How Social Mood Shapes Society* (Routledge, 2024), a rigorous examination of mood-driven social dynamics. His latest book, *Waves of Change: A Study of Social Mood* (2024), offers a more personal and wide-ranging reflection on the cycles that guide human culture and history. Ketovuori has lectured internationally across Europe, Asia, and North America, earning a reputation for challenging conventional thinking and connecting ideas across disciplines

Framespotting

Changing how you look at things changes how you see them

Laurence & Alison Matthews

A punchy, upbeat guide to framespotting. Spot deceptions and hidden assumptions; swap growth for growing up. See and be free.

Paperback: 978-1-78279-689-3 ebook: 978-1-78279-822-4

Is There an Afterlife?

David Fontana

Is there an afterlife? If so, what is it like? How do Western ideas of the afterlife compare with Eastern? David Fontana presents the historical and contemporary evidence for survival of physical death.

Paperback: 978-1-90381-690-5

Nothing Matters

a book about nothing

Ronald Green

Thinking about Nothing opens the world to everything by illuminating new angles to old problems and stimulating new ways of thinking.

Paperback: 978-1-84694-707-0 ebook: 978-1-78099-016-3

Panpsychism

The Philosophy of the Sensuous Cosmos

Peter Ells

Are free will and mind chimeras? This book, anti-materialistic but respecting science, answers: No! Mind is foundational to all existence.

Paperback: 978-1-84694-505-2 ebook: 978-1-78099-018-7

Punk Science

Inside the Mind of God

Manjir Samanta-Laughton

Many have experienced unexplainable phenomena: God, psychic abilities, extraordinary healing, and angelic encounters. Can cutting-edge science actually explain phenomena previously thought of as 'paranormal'?

Paperback: 978-1-90504-793-2

The Vagabond Spirit of Poetry

Edward Clarke

Spend time with the wisest poets of the modern age and of the past, and let Edward Clarke remind you of the importance of poetry in our industrialized world.

Paperback: 978-1-78279-370-0 ebook: 978-1-78279-369-4

Readers of ebooks can buy or view any of these bestsellers by clicking on the live link in the title. Most titles are published in paperback and as an ebook. Paperbacks are available in traditional bookshops. Both print and ebook formats are available online.

Find more titles and sign up to our readers' newsletter at www.collectiveinkbooks.com/non-fiction

Follow us on Facebook at www.facebook.com/CINonFiction